LAURA ASHLEY

Decorating with Paper & Paint

LAURA ASHLEY

Decorating with Paper & Paint

A ROOM-BY-ROOM GUIDE TO HOME DECORATING

SUSAN BERRY

Special photography by Jan Baldwin

CROWN TRADE PAPERBACKS
NEW YORK

First published in the United Kingdom in 1995 by Ebury Press
Random House, 20 Vauxhall Bridge Road, London SW1V 2SA

Published by Crown Publishers, Inc., 201 East 50th Street, New York, New York 10022.
Member of the Crown Publishing Group.

Random House, Inc. New York, Toronto, London, Sydney, Auckland

CROWN TRADE PAPERBACKS and colophon are trademarks of Crown Publishers, Inc.

Manufactured in Great Britain by Butler and Tanner Ltd, Frome, Somerset

Library of Congress cataloging-in-publication data is available on request.

Project Editor: Cindy Richards
Edited by Alison Wormleighton
Designed by Christine Wood
Special photography by Jan Baldwin
Styling by Sue Pitman
Illustrations by Kate Simunek
Picture research by Kate Duffy

ISBN: 0-517-88228-0

10 9 8 7 6 5 4 3 2 1

First American Edition

Contents

Introduction

Decorating our homes has become increasingly important over the past 15 years. Everyone's tastes have developed and decorating has become a form of self expression, revealing the character of the owner.

Laura Ashley has been in the vanguard of this trend, bringing sophisticated decorating materials and ideas to the High Street and into people's homes. What better authority could there be to advise on decorating with paint and paper than the company which has for the past 25 years produced over 50 new patterns every year for wallpaper, drape and upholstery?

Although interested in decorating, not everyone may be confident about where to begin, what will work and how to achieve the desired effect oneself. This book examines the use of colour, light and space, the effect of stripes and textures and the techniques for applying wallpaper and various paint finishes.

The design ideas range from the traditional to the more individual and sometimes quirky, enabling you to create original ideas of your own based upon those in the book.

The chapters are helpfully arranged room by room. Each one opens with an inspirational photograph of an interior designed by us especially for the book. Full of accessible decorating ideas and styling details, it is followed by step-by-step advice on how to create the effects shown. This book will inspire you, boost your confidence and give you the *savoir faire* necessary to make your home as good as our imagination.

Emma Ashley

From the simplest combinations of paint and paper (in this case Laura Ashley's Normandy Rose pattern) and taupe paintwork shown here, you can create fresh, decorative effects for any room in the house.

CHAPTER ONE

Setting the Style

Decorating a room is the fastest way to improve it dramatically, and there is now a wonderfully wide choice of paints and papers on the market. Although being able to visualize the total effect can be one of the most difficult aspects for any amateur home decorator, even total novices can achieve remarkably professional results with the help of some good ideas and practical advice.

The starting point for any decorating scheme is to decide where your taste lies. The concept of taste and style fascinates people, but few have a clear idea of what they really mean by these terms. What it appears to boil down to is knowing how to put things together, rather than the ability to recognize the worth of any one object. People with an instinctive sense of style, or inherently good taste, manage to refrain from introducing unpleasantly jarring elements into a design. The combination of elements can be eccentric, but each one has to make some kind of contribution to the overall picture. It is critically important, therefore, to know what you like. An easy way of discovering this is to thumb through magazines, catalogues, and illustrated books, marking any interiors and colour schemes that particularly appeal to you.

This quirky paint scheme works extremely well with the traditional look of the house, adding unexpected interest to the walls and emphasizing the handsome architectural features – the high, deep fireplace and large Georgian window. It also provides an excellent contrast with the dark wood floors and furniture, bringing more light into a dark room. Picking out the paintwork, in a dark colour, is in keeping with the period tradition but looks contemporary when used with the wacky paint effect.

ASPECTS OF COLOUR

For many people, the key is colour. Whether we realize it or not, colour affects our moods in a variety of ways. There has been considerable research done into the psychological effects of colours, the fruits of which have been well documented, but the findings can be misleading. Certain colours are now known to have specific psychological effects – blue is deemed a soothing colour, red a stimulating one, yellow an energizing one. They also have an effect on the look of a room, not just in terms of cosiness but in the apparent size too. Red, orange, and yellow appear to advance and so make a room look smaller, while blue and violet seem to recede and therefore make it appear more spacious. But before you become too swayed by this, consider how much a colour can vary. Red, generally regarded as a "warm" colour, can become a lot less warm when blue is added to it, while blue – a "cool" colour – can be less cold-looking if it contains yellow. Also, of course, a cool blue room can be warmed up with, say, pink fabrics and furnishings.

In addition, the light that a room receives affects the way the colour on the walls appears. The light in a west-facing room is warmer and more golden than that in an east- or north-facing room. The latter is generally regarded as offering the purest white light, hence the choice of north-facing studios by painters.

When trying to determine the colour scheme for a room, take into account not only the direction in which the room faces, but also the function of the room: is it for eating, sleeping, entertaining, relaxing, washing, or cooking? How much time will you be spending in it? In a living room, you may well decide that opting for a strong colour is not a good idea, as it would dominate your life too much, whereas the same intensity of colour would be no problem in a bathroom. Similarly, if you use the bedroom just as a place to sleep, rather than as a bed-sitting room or bedroom-cum-study, then you can afford to be a bit bolder. Here, though, you should also consider carefully whether a low-key scheme might be more relaxing last thing at night.

The proportions of the room must be taken into account when choosing colour schemes, since you can create all sorts of optical illusions with colour – lowering and raising ceiling heights, shortening or lengthening corridors, making long narrow rooms appear more rectangular, and so on. The rule here is that dark colours reduce apparent size, making a room look cosier, and pale colours increase it. This does not mean that every small room must be painted or papered in a pale colour, or that a cavernous room must be done in a dark colour to make it cosy, but you need to be aware of the effect.

Dividing up colour also tends to visually reduce the size of a room. A small apartment can be made to appear larger by opting for a single wall colour and uniform flooring colour throughout, but for many people, the slight reduction in apparent size that is created by opting for a different colour scheme in each room is more than offset by the increase in visual interest and variety.

Light colours such as white, as used in this bedroom, enlarge the apparent space in a room to give an airy, cool impression. Rich deep colours, on the other hand, such as reds tend to shrink the apparent space, making it look cosier. You can use these devices to alter the architecture of your house.

CONTINUITY OF STYLE

Think of a house or apartment as a series of spaces linked together. It is worth remembering that one room can be seen from another. Try to find ways in which the decor can be streamlined overall, perhaps by carrying some element through from one room to the next, whether it is the colour of the floor covering, or an aspect of the wall colours, or even the style of furniture.

Attention to detail, too, can help to create a feeling of continuity. A border or frieze, even if it is not the same design or colour, running at the same height in each of the rooms opening from each other will help to link them.

Another trick – employing the same colour scheme but reversing the way in which the colours are used – also helps to add continuity without looking boring. If you use one of the range of mix-and-match papers and paints, you can have the same pattern for a dado in two rooms, but with different colourways, as shown in the photograph opposite.

Reversing the colour combinations in adjoining rooms can have interesting effects on size and proportion too. Using the same colour palette, but with the dark colour for paintwork and walls, and a lighter paper in one room, and then in the adjoining room the darker paper in the same colour palette, but with pastel paintwork, creates interest but still gives the impression that the whole appearance has been considered.

Some houses have a strong sense of continuity throughout, despite the contents and colour schemes differing from room to room. Continuity can be achieved by using colours that, even if they do not match, certainly tone well. Today, it is not just the choice of colour that is important but how you use these colours throughout the interior. To expand the apparent space, use a similar colour palette, but create tonal variations from room to room, or use tone to shade the colour within a room, from floor to ceiling. Darker shades can be used on walls or behind shelves in an alcove, and will make a room seem cosier. Paler shades, on the other hand, open up the space and create a cooler atmosphere.

OPPOSITE A suite of rooms with a cleverly linked scheme. Yellow and blue are accepted as good companion colours, but the surprise introduction of oxblood is a successful accent when used in moderation with white. Note the use of the colours in reverse on the paint-effect trellis below the dado (chair) rails. Because the first door frame and the window frame at the end are both blue, the yellow door frame between them acts as a "mount" to the picture effect. Unconventional and informal, the colours and the paint effect combine to make a cheerful decoration scheme.

MIXING COLOURS

Finding colours, and colour schemes, that work together is probably the single most intimidating aspect of decorating for any amateur. It seems all too easy to get it wrong, which is why people so often opt for "safe" choices and well-tried colour combinations.

Some people seem to know instinctively which colours actually work best together. Many, however, including plenty of interior designers and other professionals, have overcome an initial lack of confidence regarding colour schemes through an understanding of the technical aspects of colour. Whole books have been written on colour theory, but the most important step is to learn what differentiates colours.

There are three primary colours, yellow, red, and blue. All other colours are made from mixtures of these, with the addition of white to lighten them (known as "tints") or black to darken them ("shades"). The complement of any of these colours is the one that is produced by mixing the other two. Thus, the complement of red is green (yellow plus blue), the complement of yellow is violet (red plus blue), and the complement of blue is orange (red plus yellow).

Fully saturated colours – those without any white or black added – are naturally brilliant. But putting these pure hues near colours that have been "muddied" by having black added to them produces a strange effect. The brightness and dullness, regardless of the colours used, can be disturbing. Combining colours that have been toned down to the same degree, by having similar amounts of black added, creates a more harmonious effect. You can use saturated colours with contrasting tints or shades so long as you get the balance right. You need to establish the overall dominant colour and then make the second colour a subsidiary, accent colour and use proportionately less of it. Walls could be in the dominant colour and woodwork in the subsidiary, or a sofa in the main colour and piping in the subsidiary one.

We have all been told that some colours "go" together and some do not. "Don't put red and pink together" is a common warning. But, in fact, you can put together whatever colours you like, so long as you get the tone right. The colour combinations given here include some which you might not have thought would go together, but which clearly do. The secret lies in similarity of tone. Look at those that are a mixture of fully saturated colours and those to which black has been added. You will see straightaway that the combination jars, because your eye is drawn to the brighter colour, while the one to which black has been added looks dingy in comparison. When you see the same colour next to one that is equally dingy, it looks great!

This is not to say that colour schemes ought to incorporate only

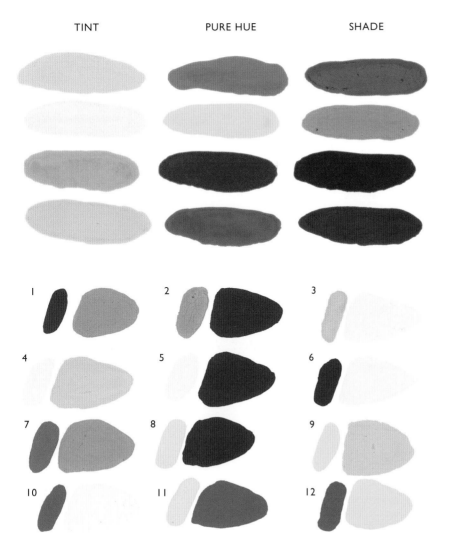

TINT   PURE HUE   SHADE

The colours here illustrate tints (colours to which white has been added), pure (fully saturated) hues, and shades (colour to which black has been added).

In the lower chart, you can see how the combinations of pure hues, tints and shades, in this case blue and yellow, combine to give different effects depending on both the size of the colour used, and the strength or density of colour.

1. Shade of blue/ shade of yellow
2. Shade of yellow/ shade of blue
3. Tint of blue/ tint of yellow
4. Tint of yellow/ tint of blue
5. Tint of yellow/ shade of blue
6. Shade of blue/ tint of yellow
7. Pure hue of blue/ shade of yellow
8. Pure hue of yellow/ shade of blue
9. Pure hue of yellow/ tint of blue
10. Pure hue of blue/ tint of yellow
11. Pure hue of yellow/ pure hue of blue
12. Pure hue of blue/ pure hue of yellow

Stripes are among the most effective forms of patterning. Elegant and simple, they never go out of fashion and therefore never date. The width of the stripe and the degree of contrast between the colours determine the effect: bright blue and white in sharply defined stripes (BELOW), painted using a plumb line and masking tape, look crisp and cool. Roller stripes (see page 131) in toning terracotta and rust (OPPOSITE) have a warmer, slightly softer appeal, in part owing to the tonal choice and in part to the less crisp paint technique.

colours of the same strength. In fact, one of the easiest schemes to work with is one based on closely related colours of different strengths. The understated elegance of a scheme incorporating tonal variations throughout the house gives a classical but up-to-date look.

Splashes of sharply contrasting colours can liven up a scheme. In the 1930s, the neutral beiges, creams, and greys favoured by decorators were often accented with colours like deep blue, coral, and maroon. Complementary colours enhance each other but can be rather overpowering in their full strength, particularly if used in equal proportions. Often, therefore, a fully saturated colour is combined with a tint of its complement. This was a common trick in Regency times, when strong reds, yellows, and greens were often used alongside tints of their complementary colours.

STYLE CONNOTATIONS OF COLOUR

Colour schemes have their own connotations, as particular colours are associated with certain styles. Interiors based on the Swedish Gustavian style make lavish use of pale, bleached woods, like lime and elm, and white and light blue painted walls and furniture. Mexican homes incorporate singing earthy colours in terracottas, apple greens, hot pinks and cerulean blues, juxtaposed in close contrast. English country-house fashion is epitomized by a wonderfully faded colour palette – old rose, peach, beige, eau-de-nil, with dimly discerned patterning. French rustic style is all Mediterranean blue and soft grey, with ochre and rust for contrast.

The colour element of ethnic styles was originally based on raw materials, since paint colours used pigments found in the soil or in plants. But now that paints and papers are coloured with chemical dyes, these colour schemes can be recreated artificially.

Certain historical periods have clear colour associations. There are the rich reds and golds of the Renaissance; the delicate pastels mixed with cream and gold of Rococo; the Georgians' deep green, stone, straw, sky blue, and bright pea green, often with chocolate brown doors and skirting boards (baseboards); the Victorians' rich reds, greens, browns, and blues; and the neutral schemes and famous all-white rooms of the 1930s.

THE IMPACT OF DESIGN

Throughout history, architects, craftsmen, and designers – such as William Kent, Robert Adam, Thomas Sheraton, William Morris, Josef Hoffman, CFA Voysey, Mies van der Rohe – have made their mark on society and on public taste. As always, designers and architects cross country boundaries. Styles move quickly backwards and forwards between Europe and North America and further afield, with ethnic designs from the Far East, the Caribbean, Africa, and Central and South America eclectically furnishing European and North American homes. Furniture and fabrics are imported from all

The pink and faded olive green used in this room are an unusual combination but work well together, the cool aspect of the green softening the heat of the pink. The colours are further unified by the toning shades of the furniture and carpets. In fact, the rugs may have been the starting point that suggested this original and refreshing colour scheme.

over the world, as we reach out to enjoy the vigour, enthusiasm, and new ideas of craftsmen and designers.

Bringing these disparate elements together under your own roof, however, can be difficult unless you remember a few basic guidelines, which will help you attain a rich and successful blend of texture, colour, and form.

If you are decorating a room, look at the elements that cannot be changed or moved: the basic room shape, the ceiling height, the shape and position of the windows and doors, the floor covering, and any architectural features. Try to work out what is good about it and what is not. Are the windows an attractive shape? Is the door solid wood, and attractively panelled? Does the room have any special features such as cornices, mouldings, dados, or picture rails to break up the flat expanse? Is there an attractive fireplace or at least a central chimney breast with alcoves either side? If the carpet is old, is there good-quality floorboarding underneath?

Elements that may not appeal to you in their existing form may well have hidden charms. A fireplace that is covered in flaking paint could reveal a wonderfully satiny finish when this is scraped away and buffed up. A door covered in layers of paint may be made of good solid oak or pine. Dull floorboards could take on a new lease of life if they are painted, limed, or stained, provided they are in reasonable condition. Old kitchen cupboards can be renovated, either by adding new wooden fronts or by painting the old fronts in more sympathetic colours and textures.

The furniture deserves the same constructively critical eye. A dilapidated old kitchen dresser could be renovated into a really attractive piece of furniture. An unremarkable chair could be given new interest with a special paint technique. Train your eye to look at the overall shapes of the furniture, and don't be distracted by chipped paint or orangey varnishes.

Paint and paper provide the opportunity to revamp a room – or an entire home – without vast expenditure. Through a carefully chosen, well thought out colour scheme, they can be used to bring together disparate elements to create a stylish and harmonious look that reflects your own personality and tastes.

ABOVE Extra interest is added to an otherwise unremarkable cornice with a handpainted frieze which, when viewed from a distance, adds depth and subtle colour.

OPPOSITE Balancing the proportions of complementary colours is the art of successful decorating. Here the blue is used as a cool accent to balance the warm and predominant beige. As well, if you can add an occasional point of interest, such as the checked fireplace, you instantly lift the decoration from the mundane to the special.

CHAPTER TWO

Paint

I f you go into a shop and buy a tin of paint, you probably do not think much, if at all, about what the paint is composed of. To the interior decorator, it is just paint.

But although it is now made in factories from chemically constructed ingredients, paint used to be made from entirely natural products. All that it consisted of was pigment – a naturally occurring mineral – bound into a paste with chalk and oil so it could be applied to a wall.

Different countries and regions tended to rely on the pigment found locally, and made up their own paints accordingly, which is why in France, for example, there is a predominance of certain colours on shutters and doorways. Although these paints are now factory-produced, the tradition for using those particular colours goes back to the days when it was ground up and produced by hand using local ingredients.

Among the earth pigments that are commonly used for paints are burnt sienna, a rich brown colour which comes from Siena in Tuscany, and burnt umber, a more reddish brown, from Umbria, both in Italy. The "burnt" element in each pigment is derived from roasting the raw pigment. The reddish brown known as Indian red is derived from red oxide, and was formerly found on the Indian sub-continent, hence the common name, but other sources have subsequently been discovered. Another source of pigment is the

A coat of paint can transform any room or piece of furniture in a very short space of time, giving it life, colour and interest, for remarkably little expenditure of either effort or money.

world's mineral deposits, including copper, manganese, tin, silica, and lapis lazuli. The colours of these tend to be brighter and more saturated than the earth pigments; some, however, are toxic and should be handled with care. A further group of pigments, which includes indigo, turmeric, madder, and alkanet, is plant-based, producing blue, yellow, pinkish red, and crimson respectively.

There is absolutely nothing to stop you mixing up your own paints provided you remember one key factor: oil and water do not mix and you must therefore never try to mix the two together to make paint.

The opacity, thickness, and general consistency of paint determine much of its character. With paint effects like sponging, ragging, or dragging, where you are aiming to get a "show through" effect, the consistency of the top coat of paint is critical. If it is too thick, the undercoat does not show through and the effect simply does not work. If it is too thin, you cannot handle it and it runs and drips down any vertical surfaces.

Formerly, the type of paint used for this top coat was called a glaze, and was made of a mixture of oil paint, pigment, and turpentine. Nowadays, you can buy this ready-made in the form of scumble, also known as transparent oil glaze (glazing liquid or glaze coat). This is either already tinted for you, or you can tint it yourself using artists' oil colours or universal stainers (tinting colours). It is good fun to do it yourself, but takes practice to get the appropriate shades. A very little artists' oil paint goes a surprisingly long way, and you need to be careful you do not inadvertently make the paint much darker than you intended. The simplest solution is to decide on a range of, say, three or four colours that you like a lot, and mix those up yourself. Alternatively, go for one of the less accessible ranges of paint which have been mixed up by traditional paint experts to give interesting "art" shades (see Stockists and Suppliers).

Whatever paint you opt for, try it out on a board or piece of cardboard first, to make sure that the colour it dries to fits in with the colour scheme you have in mind. This way, not only do you get a better idea of how the colour will look over a large area, but you can take the board into the room to be decorated to see how it fits with existing fixtures or furnishings.

OPPOSITE Strong colour, employed in a soft technique, creates an impression of warmth and richness. Here the deep sienna red walls have been colour-washed to create the effect of rough plaster. As a background to beams and wooden furniture, it creates a feeling of cosiness. To achieve this kind of colour, colourwash sienna red scumble glaze (glazing liquid) at least twice over an off-white base coat.

PAINTING – THE BASICS

Any surface you plan to paint must be properly prepared first. In fact, this preparation is what takes the time; the painting can often be done relatively quickly. The surface must be clean and completely free of oil or grease, and it must provide an adequate key to which the paint can adhere. In the case of gloss paint, this sometimes means sanding the paintwork down with fine-grade sandpaper so that the subsequent coat of paint will adhere to it properly.

PREPARING WALLS

Check that the plasterwork is in good condition before starting to decorate. Sound plasterwork does not give a hollow noise when tapped. Any badly blown or flawed plasterwork should be professionally removed and the walls replastered before you begin. New plaster must be left to dry – normally for around four weeks – and will then need to be primed before being painted using plaster primer, or a coat of PVA thinned with water. This seals any loose powder that might otherwise flake off from the plaster surface. If the plaster is old, but bare (unpainted), you can simply coat it with thinned-down emulsion (latex). Plasterboard needs to be similarly primed either with purpose-made plasterboard primer, or with thinned-down PVA paint.

Previously painted walls, if not cracked or peeling, can be cleaned with a strong cleaning agent such as sugar soap (TSP in the US) and water. You can use detergent, but you will then have to rinse the walls again afterwards to get rid of it. Any flaking paint will have to be removed using a paint scraper and elbow grease, because the new paint will not stick to it. Any cracks will have to be filled (see opposite). Water-stained surfaces or mould growing on walls will have to be treated with proprietary products before being painted, otherwise the stains will come through the new paint. Ask for advice on suitable products in your local hardware store.

Papered walls can be painted over if the paper is sound, well stuck down, and properly applied. With vinyl wallcovering, the top, shiny, layer is peeled off, leaving the lining intact. If the paper is peeling or torn, you will need to remove it entirely. Strip it either by hand using warm water and a paint stripper, or with a steam stripper, which can be hired and which does the job much more quickly, because it softens the old adhesive. Again, any rough or uneven surfaces will need to be lightly sanded and the cracks filled with all-purpose filler (spackle).

New walls that have not been papered before should be sized first, to make sure that they are not porous. Remove any wall fittings, marking the area when you paper over it.

Even the simplest painted walls can be given an extra dimension using interestingly contrasted colours. For the roughly plastered walls and simple woodwork in this cottage bedroom, the pale blue and green harmonize well because they have similar tonal values and contain more or less the same amounts of yellow. A similar tonal contrast could easily be achieved with pink and yellow, or mauve and beige – but be sure to pay attention to the way the colours are made up (see pages 14-15).

PREPARING TO PAINT WALLS

Before painting, you must have a clean, grease-free surface. Choose your type of paint to suit the effect you require. Vinyl silk gives a more reflective surface, emulsion a flatter one.

1 First wash the walls down to remove all grease using a little detergent. Rinse off afterwards.

2 Any small cracks should be dealt with using all-purpose filler (spackle) and a spatula. Overfill rather than underfill the cracks and allow to dry.

3 Afterwards, sand any lumps or bumps smooth using sandpaper or a sanding block.

PREPARING WOODWORK

Painted woodwork that is sound can simply be cleaned in the usual way, but if it is cracked, badly chipped, or peeling, it will have to be stripped back to the bare wood. You can remove paint quickly and without mess using a hot-air gun, but be careful not to scorch the wood by directing it for too long at one part. If you do scorch the wood, you will have to sand it down to remove the scorch marks. Alternatively, chemical strippers can be applied to the wood and left for a while to soften the paint, which is then removed with a paint stripper or shave hook. Be careful when using them to make sure you follow the manufacturer's instructions on any safety precautions, using gloves, masks, and/or goggles, as recommended. Wood that has been chemically treated should be wiped down with white spirit (mineral spirits), vinegar, or whatever is recommended to neutralize the chemical, after being stripped.

Use knotting solution on any wood knots, then prime the surface with an appropriate primer.

OPPOSITE It is an interesting idea to reverse the normal colour scheme and paint the windows, dado (chair) rails, and skirting boards (baseboards) in a dark colour, leaving the walls white. This helps to create a frame for the room and emphasizes any other good architectural features, such as these attractive double doors.

PREPARING TO PAINT WOODWORK

Before painting woodwork, you must prepare the surface properly, removing any flaking paint and creating a smooth surface on which to paint so the paint will adhere to it well.

1 Any badly cracked or peeling painted surface should be tackled by stripping the paint down to the bare wood, using a proprietary stripping medium.

2 After you have stripped the paint, sand it smooth to provide a good key for priming the surface.

3 Wash the entire area down with vinegar or whatever is recommended to neutralize any chemicals used in the stripping process.

ESTIMATING PAINT REQUIREMENTS

You will first need to estimate the amount of paint you will need for the job. The number of coats of paint required will vary according to the colour being applied (a light colour over a dark original paint base will require additional coats of paint to cover it properly) and the kind of paint being used. The can usually gives what is known as the spreading rate – the space the paint in the can will cover if applied at normal thickness (ie undiluted). Work out the total area to be covered by multiplying the length of the ceiling times the width, and the length of each wall times its height. Add the ceiling and wall totals to give the total square metreage/yardage of the room. Then, for the number of cans you will need, divide the total metreage/yardage by the amount the can will cover.

When organizing the painting of a room, you need to work in a systematic fashion. Remove all objects from walls and shelves, pile the furniture in the centre of the room and cover it with dust sheets, and protect the floor with paper, plastic sheeting or dust sheets. Paint the ceiling first, then the walls, starting with the window wall, and painting from top right to bottom left. It helps, with paint effects, to paint in smallish squares as the glazing medium often dries very quickly and it needs to be kept wet enough to work into it.

A quick way to calculate the amount of paint required is to add a and b, multiply the sum by c and then by 2, and then to this add a x b. Finally divide by the total metreage/yardage the can will cover.

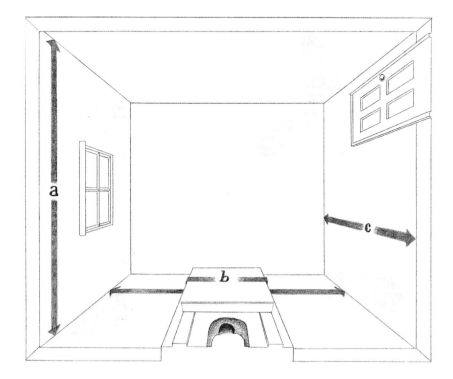

PREPARING TO PAINT

Before starting to paint, take down any pictures and ornaments. Clear the room of any furniture you can, or pile it together in the centre of the room and cover it with dustsheets or plastic sheeting. Cover the floor of the area in which you are working, and move this covering as you work around the room.

Clean the room thoroughly to remove any dust, and organize all your equipment, making sure you have rags and water or white spirit (mineral spirits) to mop up any spills straightaway. Use masking tape to cover any small areas not to be painted, and cover anything large, such as a fireplace, with newspaper and tape. Use wide masking tape to cover any nearby painted surfaces that you do not want to mark with paint – for example, the wall edge when you are painting the ceiling, or the glass windows. It is much quicker to do this than to use fine brushes to get an exact line.

Modern paints tend to drip and splash a lot less than the earlier ones, but even so you need to make sure that your painting is not marred by unsightly blobs and splatters on fixtures and fittings. Emulsion (latex) paint can be removed easily while wet using a damp rag, and oil-based paint can be removed with a rag soaked in white spirit (mineral spirits). Either type, if left to dry, will require scraping or sanding to remove so have everything you need close to hand.

PAINTING WALLS AND CEILINGS

If you are using a roller, go around all the perimeters with a fairly narrow brush, since the roller will not get into corners or close to any edge. Paint around any fittings in the same way.

Apply the paint, unless directed otherwise, in a simple criss-cross fashion, having loaded the brush with paint adequately but not to the point where it drips. Remove any surplus paint from the brush by scraping it on the side of the paint can.

Choose the appropriate size brush for the job – a large distemper brush for walls, the narrowest brush for windows. Make sure the

BRUSH PAINTING

1 Load the brush and wipe the excess off on the edge of the tin or, as shown here, a piece of string tied across the top, which prevents the edges getting covered in paint.

2 Starting at the top and working down, on a vertical surface, criss-cross the brush strokes in order to get the most even paint coverage.

3 Leave a feathered edge where you stop so that the next set of brush strokes mingles with the first without a demarcation line,

ROLLER PAINTING

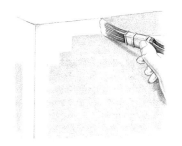

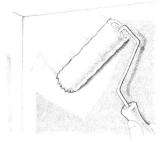

1 Paint around any edges with a narrow brush because the roller will not reach into corners.

2 Load the roller and then remove surplus paint by running the roller up and down the tray.

3 Criss-cross the roller, as you would the brush, in order to get the most even paint coverage.

brush is clean before you start and the bristles are firmly fixed to the shank. Nothing is more irritating than a brush that sheds bristles into your new paintwork.

Roller painting tends to be quicker than brush painting for large areas. You can buy various sized rollers: the slightly smaller, narrower rollers tend to be more versatile, and you can use them for roller stripes as well. Lambskin rollers are better than sponge.

LOOKING AFTER EQUIPMENT

Although you do not need a great deal of painting equipment for painting ordinary gloss or emulsion (latex), once you become interested in different paint effects you will find the equipment increases: sponges for sponging, stippling brushes, special "flogging" brushes with long soft bristles, for dragging.

It is important to buy good-quality equipment and look after it properly. How you clean the brushes and equipment depends on the paints being used. Oil-based paint and varnish are cleaned off using turpentine or white spirit (mineral spirits), while water-based paint and varnish are cleaned off with water.

When cleaning brushes that have been used for oil paint or varnish, use turpentine or white spirit (mineral spirits) and work it well into the roots of the bristles. When the brush is clean, rinse it in water and hang it up to dry. Brushes are best stored so that air can circulate around the bristles. With water-based products, simply wash the brushes out in plenty of water and dry in the usual way.

Try to store all the equipment neatly, and make sure any stencils you use are kept flat, between sheets of cardboard, as they tear easily. Stencils that have torn through wear or misuse can be mended with masking tape. Keep a notebook of any colours used, and any samples of paper, with the manufacturer's name and batch numbers on them. Have a stack of white cardboard for testing paint colours, and keep the test sheets for future reference, with the colours used.

Floors can be made infinitely more interesting with a little imagination. A stylized stencilled border that winds around the newel post at the foot of the stairs gives these pine floorboards a decorative lift (LEFT), while a geometric design has been colourwashed in subtle pastel tones (ABOVE). These colours can be achieved using purpose-made woodstains or emulsion (latex) tinted with acrylics. When colourwashing floors, score a fine line around the pattern using a craft knife (X-Acto knife) to prevent the colours from seeping into each other before they dry. Varnish the floor afterwards with matt polyurethane to make it more hardwearing.

A FLOWER FAIRY ALPHABET

FLOWER FAIRIES OF THE WAYSIDE

THE TALE OF TWO BAD MICE
THE TALE OF MRS. TIGGY-WINKLE
THE TALE OF GINGER AND PICKLES
THE TALE OF SAMUEL WHISKERS

CHAPTER THREE

Wallpaper

Wallpaper as a form of interior decoration has a relatively recent history. Prior to the advent of paper "hangings", as they were called in Elizabethan times, any ornamentation of the walls was largely achieved with woven tapestries, carved wooden panelling, or decorated plaster, and after that with fabric hangings.

Gradually, however, wallpaper came to replace textiles, and by the seventeenth century flocked wallcoverings were being produced that imitated expensive textiles such as Genoa velvet. Early in the eighteenth century they were the height of fashion, so much so that French society ladies enthusiastically removed their Gobelins tapestries so they could hang English flock papers in their place.

Hand-painted Chinese papers were fashionable among the wealthy later in the century, and these were followed by French "scenic" papers (initially hand-painted but later block-printed), which formed a continuous panorama around a room.

Other types of wallpaper had also become more popular by this time, except in the wealthiest homes, where they were only used in the servants' quarters. The papers were produced in small sheets stuck together into rolls (the dimensions of which were the basis of today's roll sizes) and then block-printed. The paper was often fixed to canvas held on battens, in the same way that textiles were hung, so that they were removable. Popular subjects for wallpaper designs

If you want to introduce pattern and decoration into your house, wallpaper is very effective. Patterns can be mixed and matched, either using some of the ranges on the market or by combining your own individual preferences, and the colour palette can vary from cool and sophisticated monochromes or pastels to bold clashing mixtures of strong contrasts.

were flowers, birds, and even human figures in landscapes in the style of the Old Masters.

In the second half of the eighteenth century, print rooms were all the rage. Monochrome engravings were pasted onto the walls of dressing rooms and studies and were framed by engraved borders linked by paper swags, bows, and other Neoclassical ornament. These sheets of printed paper could be arranged at will and were often used to decorate an entire room.

In the mid-nineteenth century, the taste for wallpaper came into its own, when the Industrial Revolution made it possible to mass-produce on continuous paper using synthetic dyes. Soon nearly every house had papered walls. The wallpapers were often textured and by the end of the Victorian era heavily embossed high-relief wallcoverings, designed to imitate leather hangings, became popular to hang on the walls beneath the dado (chair) rail, with a printed paper above, and maybe even a deep frieze above that – a fashion that has found favour again in recent years. Well-known illustrators, architects, and designers, including Owen Jones, William Morris, CFA Voysey, Walter Crane, Beatrix Potter and Kate Greenaway, produced many charming designs for wallpapers. A number of these were for children's wallpapers, which first appeared in the Victorian era and which became a popular feature of the Victorian and, subsequently, the Edwardian nursery.

Over the last two centuries, wallpapers have varied in quality from delightful but expensive hand-blocked papers, often imported from Europe, to cheaper machine-printed papers. In each succeeding era, the fashions of the period have been reflected in both the colour and the style of the wallpaper designs, from the geometric patterns of the 1930s, inspired by the Bauhaus design school, to the bright colours and realistic interpretations of the 1950s. In relatively recent years, paper, paint, and furnishing fabric were introduced in coordinated ranges by the larger companies, allowing customers to pick and choose within carefully selected mix-and-match schemes.

Today, there is a wonderful range of wallpaper available in every conceivable style, from cool, elegant stripes and traditional sprigged country patterns to bold, statement wallpaper that acts as the focal

OPPOSITE A strong Victorian look is recreated by the Owen Jones wallpaper design and by the use of the dark colours in the paintwork which match the burgundy and navy in the wallpaper border. Laura Ashley called this wallpaper reproduction "Mr Jones" in acknowledgement of the design source.

element in the decor. Most large companies produce a range of matching paints, friezes, and borders, and many also do accompanying ranges of fabrics. Try to pick and mix a little from these ranges, so that some of your own personality is embodied in the final effect.

The truly grand, hand-blocked or singularly beautiful papers that are too expensive to be used on a grand scale can be incorporated instead as decorative elements. They could be used for découpage or for covering boxes, or turned into panels.

Deciding how to use paper in a decoration scheme is more a matter of personal taste, although clearly it has a practical implication as well since it can often be used to mask less-than-perfect plasterwork. If you are attracted to decorative elements, then paper is often the best solution, but you are not obliged to use it everywhere, and quite often the most successful solution is a mixture of paint and paper.

Embossed papers in gently toning pale sapphire and ivory split this wall into two, divided by a colourwashed dado on which the same colours have been combined. This successfully unifies the scheme and covers the join between the two papers.

EMBOSSED PAPER

Although early wallpapers were designed to imitate expensive textiles, from the eighteenth century papers were also produced that simulated such materials as marble, granite, wood, leather, and plaster. By the late nineteenth century, wallcoverings with raised or embossed relief patterns had become popular, in particular Lincrusta and Anaglypta. Lincrusta – which has been taken over by Crown, who have reintroduced a wide range of Lincrusta papers and friezes – was similar to linoleum and was coated with a mixture of linseed oil, paraffin wax, whiting, and resin. This was fused to the backing paper, and the design was pressed into it to make a relief pattern using a heavy-duty roller. Laura Ashley's embossed wallpaper is still made this way.

Embossed wallpaper comes in a variety of relief patterns, many of which are designed to imitate elegant eighteenth-century plasterwork. Once hung, it can be painted with gloss or emulsion paint (latex); the relief pattern is more pronounced with a gloss coat.

Extremely hardwearing and with a timeless appeal, an embossed wallcovering makes the ideal surface below dado (chair rail) height in a hallway, and can be bought as ready-cut dado panels. It is also useful for disguising plaster that is in poor condition, though care should be taken when removing it not to inadvertently bring some of the plaster away with it.

DADOS

To prevent plasterwork from being chipped or knocked by furniture, it used to be common to line the lower part of the wall with panelling. This took the form of either softwood panelling, which was then painted over with high gloss paint, or an expensive hardwood such as oak, which would generally not have been painted. Not only did the panelling protect the wall, but it also made for a little extra insulation and warmth.

In cottages the panelling sometimes extended up to the plate rail, two thirds of the way up the wall, and this division of wall space makes an attractive country-style look for the right kind of room, such as a kitchen cum dining room.

Otherwise, the panelling was normally separated from the wall above it by a dado (chair) rail, which was usually fitted about a metre (three feet) above the floor.

You can create this kind of division of space if it suits the room. Indeed, it is still a practical solution in hallways where items like bikes and prams are inclined to make a mess of the lower part of the walls. Or, instead of wooden panelling, you can paper it with thick, embossed paper, or simply paint it with an oil-based paint that can be wiped clean. Anyone with young children in the house is well advised to think about having some sort of dado, as hand prints at low levels tend to proliferate.

DÉCOUPAGE

Highly popular in Victorian times, découpage is a technique whereby existing images on paper are cut out and stuck to a surface which is then varnished to produce a smooth finish. There is a wide range of sources for these images including catalogues, wrapping paper, fashion magazines, seed packets, and wallpaper and pattern books.

The success of découpage, however, depends on the way in which the paper cut-outs are then blended into the surface they adorn, normally by applying so many coats of varnish that they appear to be part of the surface rather than applied to it (see pages 75–6).

It is extremely effective for creating intricate hand-painted look-alikes for furniture of all descriptions, with the design ideally matching the period and style of the piece to which it is applied. Circus performers could be used on a children's toy box, while ornate rococo cherubs might adorn a delicate Louis XV-style dressing table, and military figures a Victorian campaign box.

For older furniture, it is a good idea to go for an antiqued and distressed look with the découpage images, so that the whole piece takes on a wonderfully weathered appearance.

OPPOSITE Colour and pattern are combined in a sophisticated display for this hallway, which employs not only paint effects – for the fake panelling and pillars on the walls and the three-dimensional diamonds on the dado area – but also découpage for the detailing on the door panels. Dividing the space, for both doors and walls, helps to add interest to an otherwise featureless area like a corridor.

A clever letter rack, devised from *trompe-l'oeil* wallpaper borders.

PAPERING – THE BASICS

Papering is not as difficult as it is made out to be provided you work in a logical, calm manner, and choose paper that is relatively easy to work with. Select a medium-weight paper, or one with a vinyl coating for a steamy area like a bathroom or kitchen.

Paper comes either ready-pasted or plain, or with a self-adhesive backing. Ready-pasted paper has to be soaked in water and can then be applied straight to the wall. Ordinary paper will need to be pasted on the reverse side (see page 46), and self-adhesive paper simply has its backing paper removed.

The cutting, pasting, and hanging instructions given here apply to most papers, but it's important to read the manufacturer's recommendations and follow them exactly, as they do vary.

BUYING PAPER

One of the most difficult aspects of papering can be matching any pattern repeat correctly, so choose a paper that will not give you problems for the particular room. Few rooms are square, and few ceilings level, so any obvious pattern, such as very bold geometrics, will make these faults much more visible. An overall, loose design would make this less obvious.

The colours of rolls of wallpaper do not always match, even though they may look identical. The paper is printed in batches, so it is important to check that any rolls you buy have the same batch number. If they do not, you can easily find there is a variation in the colour density, which will look very obvious once the paper is hanging. If you do for any reason have to buy paper with different batch numbers, then make certain any roll or rolls that do not match precisely are used on walls away from the window. Be sure to buy an ample amount, so that if you do not do the papering straightaway, you will not be in the position of trying to obtain more when the original batch number is no longer available. It is always useful to have some left over in case you ever need to replace a strip or two.

To work out the number of rolls required, first measure the height of the room from the skirting board (baseboard) to the coving or, if there is no coving, to the ceiling. Add an allowance of 10cm (4in) for trimming (don't skimp on this), plus the paper's pattern repeat if there is one; the total is the length of one drop. Divide that figure into the length of one roll, to find out how many complete drops you can get from one roll.

Now measure the total distance around the room (including doors and windows). Divide that figure by the width of a roll, to find how many complete drops you will need for the room.

Finally, divide the total number of drops needed by the number of drops you get per roll – that's the number of rolls you'll need. If the room has lots of obstacles like built-in cupboards, add a little extra. The chart shown here gives a guide to quantities.

This chart will enable you to calculate how many rolls of paper you require. It is based on Laura Ashley's standard roll length of 10 metres (11 yards).

Measurements around room in metres and feet (including doors and windows)

Wall height from skirting (baseboard) in metres and feet	10m 33'	11m 36'	12m 39'	13m 43'	14m 46'	15m 49'	16m 52'	17m 56'	18m 59'	19m 62'	20m 66'	21m 69'	22m 72'
2.0m-2.2m 6'6"-7'.2"	5	5	5	6	6	7	7	7	8	8	9	9	10
2.2m-2.4m 7'2"-7'10"	5	5	6	6	7	7	8	8	9	9	10	10	10
2.4m-2.6m 7'10"-8'6"	5	6	6	7	7	8	8	9	9	10	10	11	11
2.6m-2.8m 8'6"-9'2"	6	6	7	7	8	8	9	9	10	11	11	12	12
2.8m-3.0 9'2"-9'10"	6	7	7	8	8	9	9	10	11	11	12	12	13
3.0m-3.2m 9'10"-10'6"	6	7	8	8	9	10	10	11	11	12	13	13	14
3.2m-3.4m 10'6"-11'2"	7	7	8	9	9	10	11	11	12	13	13	14	15

CUTTING THE PAPER

The lengths of paper must be cut with an allowance of around 5cm (2in) at the top and the same amount at the bottom to allow for it to be trimmed. If the paper has no matching pattern, you can simply cut the lengths in advance. If you need to match the pattern, cut the first length and then measure the pattern out against it. With any patterned paper, mark the top of the paper on the back with a symbol to avoid hanging it upside down by mistake.

PASTING THE PAPER

Some paper needs only to be soaked, and with self-adhesive paper you simply peel off the backing strip. For paper that needs to be pasted you need a good working surface, such as a purpose-made pasting table or trestle table on which to work. Mix up the paste following the manufacturer's instructions. Lay the length of paper on the table, face down, with one long edge and one short edge aligned exactly with the table edges. Use a pasting brush or a roller to apply the paste. It must be applied evenly, otherwise it will bubble up once the paper has been hung. Be sure to apply it right to the edge of the paper. Be careful not to smear paste on the right side of the paper by allowing the edge you are pasting to lie just inside the edge of the table. If any paste does get onto the right side of the paper, wipe it off carefully with a damp rag while it is still wet. Wipe the table too to prevent the same thing from happening again.

Check the label to see whether the paper needs time for the paste to soak in before it is hung. If it does, paste the paper and then fold it concertina-fashion until it is ready to be hung.

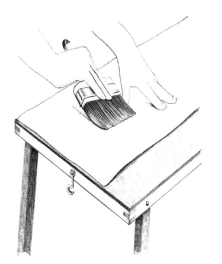

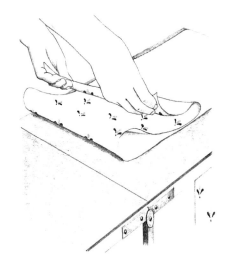

HANGING THE PAPER

First, you must ensure that the pattern is the right way up, and your pattern is both perfectly vertical and horizontal. Don't be tempted to use doorframes or windows as a guide; they are not always straight. To get a true vertical, use a plumb line, which is a leadweight on the end of a string. You pin the string to the top of the wall and when it stops swinging you mark the position on the wall to give the true vertical, which you mark with a pencil. Alternatively, rub chalk onto the string and snap it against the wall, then draw along the chalked line with a pencil; or just use a long spirit level (carpenter's level).

If you are using a paper with a strong pattern and if the room has a focal point, such as a chimney breast, then start papering at the centre of the chimney breast. The centre of the paper should be centred on the chimney breast. With other papers, start on the wall with the main window and then work around the room.

PAPER-HANGING TECHNIQUES

1 When the paper is cut, pasted, and ready to hang, fold the paper loosely, concertina-fashion, without creasing it, and take it to the wall. Align the top edge with the ceiling, leaving a 5cm (2in) overlap. Match the side edge to the plumb line to ensure it is straight, and then undo the paper, fold by fold.

2 Brush the paper out with a large soft brush from the centre to the sides, to remove any air bubbles. If any wrinkles appear, or you find the side edge is no longer aligned exactly with the plumb line, carefully pull it away from the wall beyond the problem area but not all the way to the top. Adjust the paper, then restick in the same way.

3 Brush the paper into the join between the ceiling (or coving) and the wall, mark the line with the back of the scissors, and then peel the paper back so you can cut neatly along the line. Smooth the paper back to fit and repeat the trimming procedure at the skirting board (baseboard).

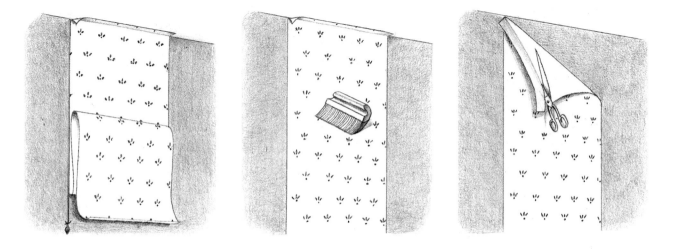

4 Take the second sheet of paper, and align it with the preceding length, being extremely careful to butt the edges up neatly. Treat in the same way as the first length.

5 Now use a seam roller, if you have one, or a rolling pin to press down the edges of the paper.

6 Most air bubbles should disappear when the paper dries, so make sure that the room is well ventilated to aid this process. If any edges spring open, repaste them carefully and press back into position. Wipe off any excess paste using a damp cloth.

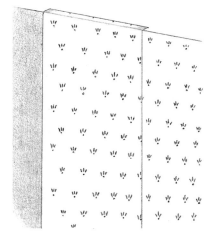

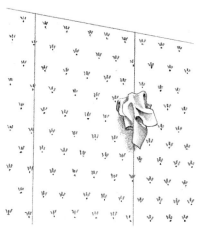

FRIEZES AND BORDERS

Friezes and borders, now back in fashion again, are the solutions for those who want a little decoration but do not want to be overwhelmed by it. Borders can be used in a host of ways, but their most successful function is to make an architectural statement – in other words, breaking up the space in specific ways to enhance the existing architectural features, or creating them in rooms that do not have them. Borders can be run around the eaves in an attic roof, around doors and windows, above skirting boards (baseboards), at dado (chair) rail height, or at cornice height. Equally, you can run the border vertically down the walls at the edges, to frame the wall, as in the photograph on page 50 (left). The secret lies in analysing the proportions of the rooms and assessing what, if anything, needs to be done to change these visually. If there is a feature you particularly wish to draw attention to, such as a fine cornice, it might be enhanced by choosing a sympathetic border pattern to run just below it.

The position of the frieze or border depends on the effect you are trying to create. You can use it to visually link the ceiling to the wall, either at the join between the two or lower down the wall, in place of a picture rail, which will have the effect of making the ceiling look a little lower in a tall room. Equally the frieze can be used at dado height, if preferred, or to create a border or edge around doorways or windows.

Paper friezes and borders can be used to give an attractive finishing touch to a papered room, but there is nothing to stop you adding a paper frieze or border to a painted room too. Borders make good links between papered and painted areas, successfully covering up the join between the two. They can also be used to bring contrasting or toning colour schemes together, providing the visual link between them. There is a good range of border and frieze patterns now available that have been planned to coordinate with specific wallpapers and fabrics, but, if you prefer, you can devise your own combinations.

APPLYING A BORDER OR FRIEZE

1 Use a spirit level (carpenter's level) to draw a pencil guideline on the wall to position the frieze or border.

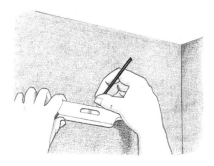

2 Paste the reverse side of the frieze carefully with wallpaper paste; or, if using self-adhesive borders, simply peel off the backing strip.

3 Align the frieze with the marked pencil line, making sure that it is accurately positioned.

4 If you need to join two pieces of frieze, butt the ends of each piece carefully and press them down with a seam roller or rolling pin.

5 To join pieces of frieze at a corner, overlap them and then cut through at a 45-degree angle with a scalpel blade or craft knife (X-Acto knife).

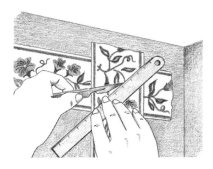

Borders can be used in a variety of ways to enhance architectural features and add interest to a room. In this scheme (ABOVE LEFT) a linked effect is created by using the same border to surround successive doorframes, in different colourways. The addition of a bow or ribbon motif at the corner points makes a focal point. A matching wallpaper and border scheme has been used in this kitchen (TOP RIGHT), the border helping to link the rather awkwardly formed shapes created when the house was altered to accommodate a downstairs cloakroom next to the kitchen. A wide stencil-pattern frieze above picture rail height (ABOVE RIGHT) will help to visually bring down the height of a tall ceiling. Here the colours not only repeat those used in the wallpaper, but tone with the objects on display on the shelves below. Where architectural features form different planes and angles (OPPOSITE), borders can be used to add definition as in this attic bedroom where they have been used vertically to define the angles between the walls as well as the angles between the wall and the ceiling.

CHAPTER FOUR

Living Rooms

This is a room in which you are going to spend a large part of your time, so the decorative scheme must be one with which you feel comfortable. Much depends on whether this room is an all-purpose family room, for eating and relaxing, or whether it fulfils more the function of a traditional drawing room.

The direction the room faces may help you to decide on an appropriate colour scheme. If it is north-facing, with a fairly cold blue light, it may benefit from a warmer-toned scheme in pinks, apricots, golds, beiges or even reds which will all help to "warm" the room. A west-facing or south-facing room, which tends to be suffused with a soft golden light, can take a cooler scheme.

The pale blues and greys of the Swedish Gustavian style are warmed by the use of bleached wood and cotton covers for the furnishings, creating an overall scheme which is easy to live with, and which has a durable appeal, since there is no single over-riding element to tire of. If you want to keep the decoration for a long period, pale, bleached-out colours are particularly useful; more strident schemes with bold patterns and strong colours will tend to date more rapidly.

Colourwashing – in which one or two thin, translucent layers of colour are applied on top of a toning base coat – is an excellent way

This delicate blue and green Gustavian-style living room has been created using colourwashed walls in two shades of blue and green, with a delicate rubber-stamped ivy pattern in dark green framing the windows. The ivy pattern was washed over with a thin coat of pale-blue emulsion (latex) to knock back the colour. The clean lines of the pale wooden furniture and country-style checks and stripes of the fabrics complete the Gustavian look.

of creating richness of colour without darkness. The use of two thin layers of colour gives the surface a glow and is much easier on the eye than a hard, single, plain colour.

The room decorated here has original panelling, but if you want to create this effect yourself, you can do so by shading the paint to imitate the three-dimensional effect of panelling.

It might be worth painting some of the furniture for the living room, and small occasional tables or chests are ideal for practising on. Stencilling or stamping are other useful decorative devices to employ not only on furniture but on the walls themselves.

If you stencil or stamp a pattern on colourwashed or sponged walls, try to ensure that it is as diffused as possible. The most attractive decorative patterns have a naturally aged appearance, which you can achieve either by employing faded colours or by washing a thin layer of the base colour paint over the finished stencil – a technique employed to knock back the ivy stamp pattern in the living room on page 52–53.

The soft furnishings – the curtains or blinds (shades) and sofa or chair covers – play a major part in determining the style of the decoration in the living room, and must be considered as part of the overall scheme. Think not only in terms of colour but of texture too. Hard, shiny fabrics will not work with soft country-style interiors – rough linens and cottons are far more sympathetic for the latter. Equally, with a classic or formal style, silks, velvets, brocades, and glazed chintzes may fit in better.

COLOURWASHING

One of the subtlest paint effects, colourwashing is an ideal technique to employ on walls where the plaster is less than perfect, particularly if you use a colourwash that is very close in colour to the base coat. The faint differences in tone resemble the shadows caused by bumps in the plaster, thereby making it hard to distinguish imperfections.

The soft, dappled nature of the finished effect is ideally suited to country-style interiors, with simple wooden furniture. It was also much used in the Scandinavian Gustavian style in shades of duck egg blue, with pale wooden floorboards and simple classical furniture. It has, in fact, long been a popular finish in cottages, where the paint used for it was distemper – a home-made paint based on whiting, glue size, and water with a thin, rather floury, very matt finish.

Colourwashing consists of a thin glaze applied over a base coat with a brush or roller, or even a cloth or sponge. Different paint experts have their own ways of working, but the effect to aim at is gentle gradations of colour, with a more watery and uneven distribution of colour than that created in normal sponged effects.

An emulsion (latex) glaze, consisting of emulsion paint (latex) thinned down with water, or an acrylic-based glaze will look much flatter and be less reflective than an oil-based glaze, which tends to have more translucency and rich depth of colour. Either finish will have much greater depth and richness of colour than a single-coloured wall, and will tend to have an attractively different appearance depending on the source and direction of the light.

Choosing appropriate colours for colourwashing is half the battle. It helps to pick colours that are close together in tone, such as soft gold over creamy yellow, because that will, in turn, produce the most subtle gradations of colour. Shades of pale blue and green over one another work well, as do pale grey and blue, apricot or yellow over warm white, and white over pale grey. You can choose to colourwash one colour or two, or even more, over a base coat.

Those tackling this technique for the first time will find it easiest to colourwash a pastel shade over a plain white base coat. This is also an easy way to revive fading white paintwork without having to redecorate the whole room.

The paint used for colourwashing is thinned a great deal more than for other broken paint effects. The recommended recipe is normally about 8 parts of water to 1 part of paint. As a result, the paint is quite difficult to work and you will need to take great care to cover all other surfaces with dustsheets while you are working.

Be warned also that the first coat of the colourwash looks tacky and uneven. With the second coat, you iron out these irregularities and give it greater depth of colour.

COLOURWASHING TECHNIQUES

METHOD 1

This technique employs a brush for the colourwashing and the glaze is simply brushed lightly out rather than being removed with a sponge (see Method 2 below).

1 Apply the base coat (emulsion or eggshell depending on whether a water- or oil-based top coat is being used) in criss-cross fashion.

2 When the base coat is completely dry, brush over a very wet glaze – eight parts of water to 1 part emulsion, or 8 parts white spirit (mineral spirits) to 1 part oil paint – in random fashion. Allow the glaze to dry.

3 Brush out a second coat of glaze in a closely related colour, going over any areas where the colour is unevenly applied.

4 Glaze with a clear polyurethane varnish if the finish is to be waterproof.

OPPOSITE Colourwashing can be strong or subtle depending on the contrast between the colours. The stronger the contrast, the less subtle the effect. Here, closely toning shades of blue and grey have been used which give just a hint of surface texture, and a very subtle play of light on the surface. If you want to strengthen the effect, go for a more pronounced colour contrast, but beware of extremely strong contrasts.

METHOD 2

This technique uses a sponge to remove the glaze and a brush to soften the effect. Work with two people, one to remove the glaze with a sponge, and the other to go over the area with a brush.

1 Apply the base coat in the same way as in step 1 above.

2 Apply the glaze. Then dip a piece of natural sponge in water or white spirit (mineral spirits) and wring it out. Work into the *wet* glaze, taking it off in a series of dabbing, rolling, and dragging movements to give an irregularly mottled finish. Rinse the sponge when it starts to get clogged with paint.

3 With a soft-bristled dry brush, smooth out the area you have worked on while it is still wet in order to blur the effect. Use large, quick random brush strokes.

GRISAILLE

This very simple form of *trompe l'oeil* (literally tricking the eye) is used to create false architectural features such as panels and door frames. Or if you are very artistic, you can create images like plasterwork urns and caryatids (pillars in the form of draped female figures).

What you are, in fact, doing is painting in false shadows and highlights to create a three-dimensional effect that tricks the eye into thinking that the surface is raised or indented.

Although grisaille was historically carried out in black and white, you could experiment with tones of another colour, adding a mixture of blue, brown, and black paint to the base colour.

GRISAILLE TECHNIQUES

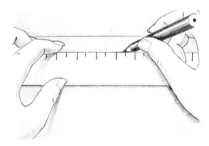

1 Use a small piece of moulding as a reference. Measure the widths of the prominent parts and recessed parts and recreate these in pencil on the surface you are working on, having first measured out the overall area.

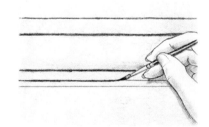

2 Using a fine artist's brush, paint in the darkest areas first in black or nearly black.

4 Finally paint in the relief areas in white. You can use this technique on coloured surfaces, mixing the colour you are using with shades of black and white as appropriate.

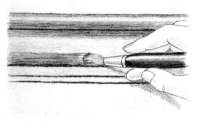

3 Now paint in the areas of mid-shade in grey.

LEFT This pretty little chest has great charm. You can create the same effect with a piece of discarded furniture by painting the overall surface with an off-white undercoat and distressed tobacco-coloured topcoat. The vase of flowers shown here has been stencilled and painted freehand to achieve the aged look. The vase itself has a three-dimensional grisaille effect, in which shading is used to imitate the actual curves of the object.

Grisaille can also be used in straight lines to create the impression of panelling, as seen on the sides of the little chest (BELOW). Although the walls in this room were genuine panels (RIGHT), you could create the same effect on plain walls using the grisaille panel technique. Darker tones are used to create the impression of a recessed area, and paler shades the more prominent parts, or parts that reflect the light. Practise on cardboard until you can achieve a realistic effect.

STAMPING AND BLOCK PRINTING

Interesting shapes and motifs can be found in the form of rubber and wooden stamps, which you can buy ready-made, and can use to print onto walls, furniture, fabrics, floors, and lampshades. If you prefer, you can cut your own stamps out of root vegetables (potato prints) or artist's linoleum.

The craft of hand-block printing has a long history: carved wooden or bone stamps were used as seals in ancient Babylon and it is still popular today in Polynesia and Africa. In West Africa, gourds are carved into simple patterns and used to decorate fabric. The very earliest dyes that were used in hand printing were made from finely ground pigments such as soot, red ochre, and various earths, mixed with oil as a binding agent.

The best effects in hand blocking or stamping are achieved with simple designs, as the chief danger is that the paint or printing ink will form unsightly blobs if too much is applied to the stamp, and the cut-out lines will fill in.

If you are cutting your own blocks out of lino or vegetables, keep the pattern very simple – geometric shapes are ideal – and make sure you cut them out cleanly and evenly with a very sharp blade, such as a craft knife. If you are making vegetable prints, you will have to allow the water to drain from the vegetable before using it. Sprinkle salt on the cut surface and let it drain for 20 minutes, then pat the surface dry with a kitchen towel.

Lino can also be cut easily using a very sharp blade and has the advantage over the vegetable blocks in that paint adheres to the surface more easily. Rub the surface down with fine-grade steel wool to ensure that the paint or ink will cling to it well.

CUTTING YOUR OWN BLOCKS

1 Mark the pattern out on the lino or vegetable block using a felt tip pen.

2 Cut around the pattern carefully, removing any areas that are to be left free of ink or paint.

3 If using lino, rub the surface of the block with fine-grade steel wool so the paint will adhere to the surface.

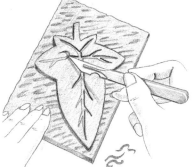

OPPOSITE Stamps are invaluable for adding decoration quickly and easily. You can buy them ready-made, as this ivy pattern was, or get a rubber stamp company (through a stationer's) to make them up from your own drawings or photographs, or make one yourself (as left). These motifs were painted in dark green, and were then washed over afterwards with diluted emulsion paint (latex).

Used in much the same way decoratively as a stencil, block printing is ideal for creating small areas of decoration to emphasize an architectual feature, such as a window enclosure, or in a panel on a door or shutter. In days gone by, hand-blocked prints were the most common form of decoration for wallpaper. The technique is still used today, and the slightly uneven quality is a much sought after finish, with hand-blocked wallpapers commanding extremely high prices. You could imitate this effect yourself, by creating something similar.

Some of the most attractive effects are those in which the printed images are created randomly, or even so they overlap. However, if you want to create a pattern on a regular grid, you will have to measure and mark out the surface using a T-square to get the blocks accurately lined up. Use

chalk to mark the positions of the blocks as it can be rubbed off easily afterwards.

For the printing medium you can use paint or printer's ink. The best paint to use is artist's acrylics, thinned with water, to which a little acrylic medium has been added so that it is the consistency of thick cream. Acrylic paint dries very quickly so do not mix more than you can use up in about half an hour. As always, keep a careful note of the colours and quantities you have used so you can remix the same colour if needed later.

When you have mixed and prepared the chosen colour, transfer it to a sheet of glass. (Glass is used because the paint or ink spreads better.) Roll it out with a small printer's roller (available from most craft shops) and then press the block into the paint. Test the effect on a sheet of paper, to see whether too much paint, or too little, is being applied, and to make sure that the consistency is neither too thick nor too runny, and the pressure on the block even. A little unevenness in the application of the print is perfectly acceptable – the aim is for it to look hand-done, not machine-finished.

The rubber stamp kit. You can buy stamp, roller, and paint complete if you wish. If not, either buy or make the stamp, then buy a rubber roller and use emulsion (latex) or coloured printing ink for the paint.

PRINTING TECHNIQUES

1 Mix the printing ink or paints to the colour and consistency required in a small dish.

2 Spread the mixture out on a sheet of glass and roll out with a printer's roller, rolling it in several directions.

3 Press the block, face down, in the mixture to cover the surface with the printing ink or paint.

4 Apply the inked or painted surface of the block to a piece of paper or cardboard and press firmly, using even pressure, taking care not to shift the weight on it. Lift the block in one clean movement. Check the resulting image. If it is not printing evenly, the surface of the block may not be completely flat or the paint may be too dry or too thick. If the image is blurring and the cut lines are filling with ink, the ink may be too runny.

5 When you are satisfied with the effect apply the technique to the surface for printing. Once the images are dry, varnish them with a water-based, matt acrylic varnish if you want to make the surface waterproof.

Warm colours, such as yellow, apricots, peaches, pinks, and reds, are particularly useful in rooms with north- or east-facing windows, to add warmth to the blue light you get in these rooms. The sharper yellow (ABOVE) contains much more blue and is therefore more acid-looking than the more peachy coloured room (LEFT), which has quite a bit of red in its yellow composition. Using off-white rather than pure white also helps to give warmth and tones down the colour

to some extent. In the strong yellow room (ABOVE) the cupboards have been painted to blend with the walls, thereby focussing attention on the contents and unifying the colour scheme at the same time. The white dado area helps to prevent this from becoming overwhelming. In the tonal-striped yellow room (LEFT), pattern has been used on both the soft furnishings and the paper frieze to add interest, and the wall colour echoes the main colour in the print motif.

ABOVE A subtle colour combination, using moss and sage greens, slate blues and cream, has added an air of calm elegance to this Edwardian-style living room. The white ceiling heightens the room's proportions, in keeping with the period feel.

RIGHT People tend to be nervous about using strong colour, but it can work extremely well. Here, the hot lacquer-red of the walls has been calmed with the cool, pale green dragged woodwork and frieze. The strong colour provides an excellent backdrop for the Indian pictures and furnishings. The Indian theme is made complete by the Kashmiri crewelwork curtains.

CHAPTER FIVE

Kitchens

Kitchens need decorating more frequently than any other room in the house, especially now that the kitchen also often doubles up as the family room. Gone are the days of the streamlined, minimalist, galley-style kitchen, often occupying the smallest space in the house. Nowadays, even in small flats and houses, rooms are often knocked together to make a large kitchen cum living room which has a warm, friendly, and informal atmosphere. In newly designed kitchens, freestanding furniture has often replaced made-to-measure kitchen units, and with it a decorating style that is much more eclectic, with a mixture of furniture in different colours and finishes.

To many people who opted wholesale for pine furniture in the 1980s, the techniques of painted finishes and ageing and distressing are very useful, since they allow you to give an excitingly different look to the kitchen without spending a fortune.

Pine dressers can be painted a deep sea green or French country blue, rubbed down so that the wood glows through, and then waxed to produce an apparent patina of age. Walls can be colourwashed or stippled in soft ochres, terracottas, or grey-blues. Floors, if wooden boards, can be stained and limed (pickled) to blend in with the overall colour scheme. Wood, and also lino and vinyl tiles, give warmth and comfort, while the cold surface of terracotta tiles makes them less suitable in cooler climates.

This kitchen is kept light by using white on the skirting (baseboard) and doors, while the green in the engraved vegetable wallpaper is picked up by the paint on the dresser in the corner and, in a darker tone, the range. A frieze fixed just below ceiling height helps to provide visual continuity in what might otherwise be a disturbing mix of different planes. The aim in this kitchen is to create continuity so that your eye glosses over the difference.

When choosing colour schemes for a room, try to ensure that they work well with any favourite ornaments you wish to display. It often pays to take a particular collection – jugs, plates, pictures – and use their colours to guide your final choice. This simple, patterned paper works well in both colour and style with the traditional patterned china of the jugs. The green shelf anchors the whole scheme.

The country look – whether English country-house, American folk, or French provincial – all hangs on the use of natural, rather than synthetic, materials such as wood, stone, and brick. If your kitchen has existing fittings which are not real wood, you can give it a more natural appearance, either by simply fixing new wooden doors to the old base units or, if they can be painted, by cheating and using a wood-effect paint finish on the existing cupboards.

Whatever surface you opt for in the kitchen must be steam- and grease-resistant. In other words, use an eggshell paint finish, or one of the modern acrylic paints, and use vinyl or vinyl-coated wallpaper.

Since the kitchen will inevitably have its own array of china, glassware, and cooking utensils, much of it on display, the colour scheme will look best if it provides a backdrop for this showcase of colour rather than competing with it. Avoid too much obvious pattern. A gently textured paint finish, such as sponging, stippling, or ragging, is ideal, as is the even more muted colourwashed finish. (see pages 54–56).

If you are going to paint some or all of the furniture or fittings, you need to plan out the colour scheme fairly carefully so that it looks pleasantly natural but not bitty. One way to vary the colours without creating too jazzy an effect is to use toning colours, with perhaps the odd contrast to add some life to the overall scheme. These could be soft, pale eau-de-nil sponged walls, with deeper green antiqued cupboards, and the occasional touch of a contrasting colour such as a deep Indian red for chair cushions or blinds, picking up a warm, rusty-red quarry-tiled floor. The softly toning blues, beiges, and off whites of the Scandinavian Gustavian style would work well in a kitchen where the china, for example, was delicate country flowers. But if the accessories are brilliant hand-painted earthenware, then you may find that a colour scheme like the brilliant blues and yellows of Monet's kitchen at Giverny makes a better backdrop.

Fabric, in the form of blinds, table covers, throws over easy chairs, and squab cushions, helps to soften an otherwise rather severe kitchen, as do small amounts of pattern – a stencilled border around a window frame or door, perhaps, or painted panels in a chest or shutters. If you have opted for the rather neutral, Swedish style, make sure that any pattern is not markedly strident, or it will simply dominate the backdrop and unbalance the decor. Strongly contrasting primary colours on walls and furniture can be offset by equally strong brightly coloured stripes or checks, say, for the fabric. You can buy striped and checked cotton very cheaply or you can paint fabrics (see page 89).

ANTIQUING AND DISTRESSING

Antiquing and distressing involves giving a piece of furniture an aged appearance by rubbing away at the layers of paint, so that previous coats are revealed. If you have visited southern Europe and admired the effect of weathered paint, you can recreate this effect quite easily if you wish.

One of the great virtues of paint effects is that they can be used to give a piece of furniture character that it does not naturally possess. Anyone who acquired stripped pine furniture with which they have gradually become bored can, for a small outlay of money and a rather larger one of time, turn these pieces into something of real beauty by painting them, and then distressing the paint finish.

There are various methods of antiquing a piece of wooden furniture, and one of the simplest is that used for the dresser shown on the previous page.

All you have to do is to paint the dresser with a coat of fairly thick paint. Those produced with a mixture of emulsion (latex) and PVA (see Stockists and Suppliers) are ideal, but, failing that, use ordinary emulsion paint, and then give it a second coat in a different colour. Once that has dried, you simply rub away at the finished layer of paint with steel wool to reveal the underlying paint, and even the wood beneath that. To seal the surface of the dresser, varnish with polyurethane gloss or simply wax it, rubbing the wax in with fine-grade steel wool, and then leaving it for 20 minutes or so before buffing it up with a duster.

When you rub away the paint, try to imitate the natural wear that occurs with the passage of time. Rub corners and leading edges or areas where the piece is handled a lot, so that the wear marks look as authentic as possible.

Colours that look good distressed in this way are dark green over mid-brown, dusty blue over antique white for a Swedish look, and Indian red over brown, as well as white over ochre. Or you can use contrasting colours that feature in the colour-scheme of your room.

If you use one of the special darker-tinted waxes over it afterwards, you will give it that slightly dirty look which is counter-acted by the sheen of the polish, so that it looks genuinely old.

Another technique for a similarly aged look is crackled paint. In this you use a layer of crackle medium, like the filling in a sandwich, between two layers of emulsion (latex) paint which then causes the top coat to peel. If done carefully, it looks very effective, particularly if you choose soft colours – creams, dull greens and blues, and soft brick reds. Wax it afterwards for a more authentic finish.

OPPOSITE A pine dresser gained a new lease of life by being painted in a rich grass green, and then rubbed back to reveal the wood in places, giving it an aged appearance. Waxing with dark antique wax afterwards will enhance the antiqued appearance. Concentrate the rubbing away at the prominent parts – corners, handles, and protruding parts – so it looks like genuine wear and tear.

ANTIQUING TECHNIQUES

1 Prepare and prime the wood if necessary. On old pine furniture, remove any wax polish by rubbing with fine-grade steel wool soaked in white spirit (mineral spirits), and then rub down with vinegar.

2 Apply a base coat of dark brown paint fairly thickly without worrying too much how even it looks – it will be covered by the subsequent coat(s).

3 When the base coat is dry, apply the second coat – your chosen finished colour for the piece.

4 Rub over the piece unevenly and roughly with antiquing wax.

5 Using coarse-grade steel wool, selectively rub away the paint to reveal the layers beneath.

6 Buff it up with a soft cloth.

DÉCOUPAGE

Used in past centuries to decorate fine furniture, this popular Victorian pastime for ladies of leisure has recently enjoyed a revival. Basically, it involves sticking cut-out pictures onto a surface and then varnishing over them to make them look as though they were actually painted on the surface. Hence the French name "découpage", meaning to cut out. Depending on the images used, you can achieve different effects, from Victorian collage to exquisite hand-painting, but equally you can cover screens, toy boxes, etc.

For practising, it is fun to use some simple household objects – trays, wastepaper bins or hat boxes for example – and turn them into interesting *objets d'art*.

You need to find a source of good material to cut out. In the kitchen overleaf, the images from the kitchen wallpaper were simply cut out and stuck to the tray. Wallpaper is a good source, as are calendars, wrapping paper, catalogues and seed packets but there are actual books printed specially for découpage which have recreated many of the old images from Victorian journals and cut-out books. Another solution is to photocopy an image from a book or from fabric, and then handcolour it yourself. The art is in the way these cut-out elements are composed to form an overall picture.

In the olden days, to give the smooth, glassy surface that imitated painted furniture, it took about 20 coats of varnish over the stuck-down images and sanding down between every layer or two. You can now buy special varnish for découpage that requires far fewer coats to produce the same excellent surface. If you do not mind how smooth the final result is, then you can get away with just a couple of coats of ordinary polyurethane varnish.

RIGHT This close-up of a tray shows how the cut-out images from the wallpaper have been combined to make a vivid and unusual découpage, but without the smooth, glassy surface commonly associated with the technique. Here, no attempt is made to resemble painting: it is a much more homely version, particularly suitable for kitchen use.

OPPOSITE The wall behind the dresser was given a striking treatment in bold green and white stripes, painted accurately using a plumb line and masking tape to divide the stripes. This effect makes the dresser look less traditional and more up-to-date.

DÉCOUPAGE TECHNIQUES

1 Cut the images out very carefully using either scissors or a scalpel and a cutting board. Be careful not to leave any telltale outline.

2 Check that the surface you are planning to stick them to is clean, and if necessary paint the surface first and allow this to dry.

3 Arrange the images in the pattern you require and then stick them down with PVA glue, making sure all the edges are firmly stuck. A damp sponge is ideal for smoothing the cut-out images down to prevent air bubbles, and removing any traces of glue.

4 When the glued images are dry, coat the whole area with a thin coat of varnish, using a varnish with a slight ochre or brown tint if you want an antique look. When this is dry, revarnish it. Allow to dry, then sand. Carry on doing this, sanding after every second coat until you are satisfied with the overall effect.

OPPOSITE **The images for this small découpaged tray were cut out from left-over ends of the wallpaper rolls used to decorate the kitchen, and then pasted onto the tray in an all-over, random pattern. If you prefer, you can create a single image in the centre of the tray, or repeat the image as a border, or place it in each of the four corners of the tray.**

Subtle, soft colour combinations are
used too rarely in kitchens, where the
tendency is to go for bright contrasts.
Colourwashing, provided it is varnished
afterwards to cope with steam and
condensation in the kitchen, is an
excellent treatment for kitchens. These
beautifully toned terracottas, browns,
and beiges redolent of Tuscan kitchens
make a perfect foil for copper and steel
kitchen equipment, which can look
harsh and clinical against bright
surroundings. The pine columns flanking
the doorway and supporting the
worktops make this kitchen even more
interesting and distinctive.

ABOVE Stencilled fish form a decorative motif for the painted base of this handsome kitchen table. The base echoes the colour scheme used for the walls and cupboards, and links the table with the rest of the room.

RIGHT Elegant bird stencils form the central panels to these wooden kitchen cupboards, with stencilled borders providing additional decoration. The warm red and blue tones contrast well with the pale beige of the cupboards, without looking too strong or obvious.

CHAPTER SIX

Bedrooms

Of all the rooms in the house, the bedroom probably expresses the personality of the owner most closely, and the decorative scheme will be, to some extent, an expression also of lifestyle. Colour can be used to create mood and atmosphere and here the deeper colours – glowing crimson and deep indigos – may well help to create a warm and womblike feel to the room, if that is what is desired. Paler colours will make a small, cramped bedroom feel more spacious. It will also make one that has little natural light less gloomy, as many bedrooms suffer from relatively small or badly placed windows. Paler colours do not have to be boring, particularly if you pick slightly unusual or "sharp" colour combinations – acid greens and pale pinks or apricots; cobalt blue and yellow; lilac and coffee.

Bedrooms can be sumptuous, with a statement wallpaper perhaps, dark paintwork, and rich bedhangings; or pretty, with pastel, sprigged prints and papers, and delicately sponged or dragged furniture. The sheer quantity of fabric in the bedroom tends to create a softer atmosphere than in any other room in the house and if you want to play on this, you can. Be careful, however, not to go overboard. Too many frills, flounces, and furbelows give a rather cloying appearance to the room; if you are using pretty pastel colours, go for a simpler fabric effect. If you are using colour schemes like maroons, bottle greens, browns, or black and white,

Paper looks particularly good in large square rooms with high picture rails. Here, contrasting pinks and greens have been used for the colour scheme, with the walls papered in a small white geometric print on pale green, and the area above the picture rail papered a pink check. Bed linen from a coordinated range, in a pink and green floral and check pattern, completes the look. Green and pink are good partners when used in similar tones, where the green counteracts the potentially sickly pink. This pink carries a lot of blue so can be quite cold, but the green carries a lot of yellow so is a great foil for it.

then you can afford more richly draped fabric and more heavily patterned papers. It is all a question of balance. Too clinical and severe, and it fails to satisfy the emotional needs; too pretty and feminine, and the scheme will lack elegance and sharpness.

The bed is normally the central focus and the fabrics chosen for the covers and bedlinen will tend, to determine the colours of the other surfaces.

It is often a good idea to pick out a colour or theme from the furnishings in the room to create the scheme, perhaps using the pattern to create your own stencil, for blinds (shades), curtain or pelmet (valance) borders, or lampshades. In the bedroom shown on page 82, the simple check-pattern paper used for the area above the picture rail was copied freehand onto plain white lampshades, an effective trick for uniting the colour scheme.

DRAGGING

To create soft and attractive surfaces that are relaxing and easy on the eye, employ some of the broken paint effects that form part of the home decorator's repertoire. Dragging is a particularly useful finish for woodwork, since it prevents it from looking too hard and reflective. If you want to opt for a country style bedroom, plain white bedroom cupboards can be transformed by dragging them in a pastel colour such as pale green, blue or apricot over white. Or paint a simple coloured border onto a white cushion.

If you look more closely at a painted surface, you realize that some surfaces absorb light and others reflect it. This degree of absorbency or reflectivity makes a great deal of difference to the atmosphere of the room. A glossy surface is crisp and hard-edged, whereas a matt surface tends to produce a much more subtle, softer feeling.

Dragging is a useful technique because it provides a glossy finish without the hardness normally associated with it. Dragging is exactly what it sounds like – one coat of paint is literally dragged over the undercoat using a soft-bristled brush, so that the top surface of paint leaves faintly irregular vertical lines on the base coat.

OPPOSITE This view of the room demonstrates how the high ceilings have been visually lowered using a contrasting paper above the picture rail. The feature fireplace has been dragged in pale green over white. The whole effect is updated traditional.

You can use the technique on walls or on woodwork, although it is more commonly used on the latter. To persuade the top coat of paint to slide easily and smoothly over the base coat, the latter really needs to be the type with a sheen, such as an eggshell or silk, and ideally an oil-based one. The top coat used is a tinted glaze, which in the old days used to be made up from linseed oil, turpentine and whiting but nowadays can be bought ready-prepared in any good paint shop, usually under the name of scumble glaze (glazing liquid). For a more subtle dragging effect, use emulsion paint (latex).

With the advances in paint technology, you can now also buy acrylic-based glaze, which has the advantage that it is water-based so you can clean your brushes out in water. This type of glaze has to be applied over a water-based undercoat, such as an acrylic eggshell or emulsion silk finish. If you discuss it with any experienced painter they will tell you that acrylic is a bit like a poor man's paint, in the sense that it does not give the richness or luminosity of finish that you get with oil-based glazes. It also dries much faster, which you might think was convenient, but for paint effects it is not a desirable characteristic, since you have to keep the paint wet as long as possible so that you can work it with your dragging brush, sponge, or whatever. However, if you can work with a partner – one of you applying the glaze while the other drags it with the brush – it is perfectly effective, and certainly quicker and a lot less smelly, than oil-based paints and glazes.

As with all paint techniques, dragging needs to be carried out with confidence. As this isn't the hallmark of someone nervously experimenting with a new technique, it pays to practise on a large piece of cardboard first, or on a wall that you then repaint. The most common problem is a build-up of glaze where you stop for any reason. Ideally, you should drag down the wall or piece of furniture from top to bottom in one long movement, but this is more or less impossible so the solution is to stop two-thirds of the way down, and then drag from the bottom up for the other third, feathering the paint where it meets. Be careful not to stop at exactly the same point on each downward stroke, or you will get a slight irregularity, which will form a line around the room or in one place on the furniture.

USING COLOUR IN DRAGGING

Dragging is often done as a pastel glaze over a plain white surface, or a deeper colour over a pastel base, so that the pale base coat shows through the dragged glaze, giving it a pleasantly light finish. If you are inexperienced, pick a glaze that is not too far removed in colour from the base coat, because then the brush marks, and any irregularities in them, will not show up as much. A pastel green, blue or beige glaze over a white base coat, or lilac over grey, would be quite easy to apply.

Since the scumble or glaze that you buy comes in a fairly limited range of colours, you will be much better off tinting your own. If you are buying oil-based glaze, tint it with artist's oil colours or universal stainers (tinting colours) and if you are buying acrylic glaze use acrylic paints. There is a much bigger range of artist's oils than universal stainers (tinting colours), but the latter are easier to mix in since they are very runny. Be careful, since a tiny amount goes a surprisingly long way and once you have coloured the paint you cannot uncolour it. Add it drop by drop until you have something approaching the colour you want, and then brush it out on a card to see what you think of the colour it dries to. With artist's oils, you will have to thin the colour with a little white spirit (mineral spirits) before adding it to the paint.

If you become proficient at dragging, you can try out all sorts of interesting colour combinations, using a coloured base coat to provide extra interest. Not everything works, so do test it out first and mix up only small amounts of colour at a time.

You should also take note of any colours that you mix, and the proportions used, since it will be impossible otherwise to mix up the same colour again. Even if you do this, the colour may not be exactly the same, so, to be safe, always make too much top coat.

If the colour runs out halfway through the job, try to gauge it so that you complete at least one wall, since if the colour varies from wall to wall it will not be so noticeable. Because the colour is not flat, it as not as obvious as with an all-over one-colour paint that the shade has changed a little. It looks more like a trick of the light.

This dragged fireplace has employed exactly the same colours as those used in the wallpaper surrounding it: sage green and white. The sage green glaze has been dragged over the white eggshell base coat, giving a paler show-through of colour and softening the overall effect.

DRAGGING TECHNIQUES

1 Paint the base coat, using an oil-based eggshell (mid-sheen) or silk emulsion (latex velvet).

2 Tint the glaze if necessary to the required colour, and start to apply to the wall with up and down strokes, criss-crossing the brush strokes in X-shapes. If you are working on your own, work in manageable sections.

3 Using a long, soft-bristled brush, ideally a purpose-made dragging brush, and working from the top downwards, smoothly and evenly bring the brush down through the glaze while the latter is still wet.

4 If you cannot drag the surface in one long movement, start at the top and drag most of the length and then go to the bottom and drag upwards to meet the completed section. Feather the join by brushing gently into it.

5 If you wish to create a more hard-wearing finish, such as in a bathroom or kitchen, varnish the surface with clear matt polyurethane varnish.

A close up of the fireplace shows the dragging technique more clearly. The result is a soft, streaky finish that is less hard-looking than gloss paint yet is more durable than emulsion (latex). Dragging helps to visually break up large areas of woodwork, and looks best in fairly soft pastel shades.

HAND PAINTING ON FABRIC

It is surprising how nervous most adults are of using paint in anything other than the conventional way – particularly as children are prepared to experiment with any surface and any medium!

With lampshades, unless you opt for plain colours, it is rare to find exactly what you want in colourways that go with your decorative scheme, unless you buy shades that are part of a coordinated range.

To give your room a touch of individuality, it is actually very easy to paint a plain white or parchment shade with emulsion (latex) or acrylic paint to give really good results, provided you keep the pattern simple. You can also use stencils very effectively on lampshades, though you need to go for fairly small patterns because manipulating the stencil card around the conical base of the lamp can be tricky. A random all-over stencil pattern is easier to apply than a more formal border, where the edges have to meet successfully. Acetate stencils *can* bend over the curve of a lampshade.

If you want to paint stripes or checks on a lampshade, masking tape can be used to keep the paint colours separate and straight.

A pair of very basic cardboard lamp-shades have been given a finish of simple checks painted straight onto the shade with vinyl matt (flat latex) paint.

HAND-PAINTING TECHNIQUES

1 If the surface is porous, paint a coat of thinned-down PVA over it to size it and seal it.

2 If desired, mask off stripes or checks with tape. Apply the emulsion (latex) paint in broad stripes or checks over the surface.

3 Apply the second colour, if required, between the first colours to make a plaid effect.

4 Varnish the finished shade with matt polyurethane varnish to seal it, so that it is wipable.

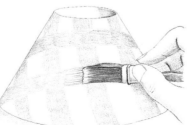

COVERING BOXES

Using odds and ends of wallpaper to cover boxes or as a decorated frieze along a shelf edge is a good way of creating a unified look in a room. If the wallpaper has no backing, it is easier to use a spray adhesive, but you could use PVA (white) glue instead if you wish. Self-adhesive wallpaper or ready-pasted wallpaper can be dealt with in the normal way. Decide on an appropriate pattern – it will look prettier if you use more than one paper to create borders and edgings, such as a small amount of matching frieze around the lip of a hat box lid.

BOX-COVERING TECHNIQUES

1 Measure the box and redraw these measurements on the back of the paper. Add on ½in (12mm) at each side to turn back over the edges. Cut the paper pieces out using sharp scissors or a scalpel.

2 Paste the reverse side of the paper with wallpaper paste, spray adhesive, or PVA (white) glue and roll it carefully round the box. Start at the centre of each piece and wipe the surface out to the edges with a dampened sponge to remove any wrinkles. Snip the extra paper at regular intervals, to aid turning it back over the edges.

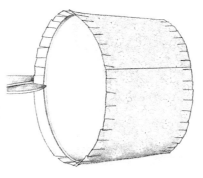

3 Turn the snipped edges over the box and paste down.

4 Cover the lid in the same way. Then cut a strip to border the lid, and paste on carefully.

OPPOSITE The exciting ranges of coordinated papers, friezes, and borders can be used to great effect to decorate boxes, like these hatboxes. Always use the manufacturer's recommended wallpaper paste.

Neutral colour schemes are often the most effective, and will certainly help give a room a spacious feel. Both these schemes use the warm yellow/apricot/ beige colour range. In this room, (RIGHT), the walls have been sponged and colourwashed in cream with a hint of apricot. A wheatsheaf ribbon border has been stencilled very delicately in a slightly darker shade at ceiling height and outlining the window frame. To achieve this antique effect, you may need to colourwash the wall after stencilling, using a thinned-down emulsion (latex) paint in a slightly darker tone of the same shade. This galleried room (ABOVE) uses a slightly warmer, more pinky apricot for the stippled walls, while the ornate plaster cornice has been antiqued in shades of grey, the colour scheme reflected in the bed linen.

TOP This Chinese-style wallpaper, with branches of exotic flowers and birds, makes a strong impact and is known as a statement wallpaper in the trade. The decorative scheme will be organized around it, precisely because it is very dominant. Although it lends itself well to large, traditional, formal rooms with elaborate furnishings, it can also be very successful in a small room. The rest of the furnishings and the colour scheme can be kept simple.

LEFT An example of how to choose a stencil successfully. The fine curls and loops of the antique metal bedhead have been echoed in the curling scroll form of the stencilled border, in a similarly dark paint on a white ground.

RIGHT With its limewashed (pickled) wood floor and its cream and blue wallpaper, the Swedish Gustavian-style bedroom shown here is simple yet not plain. Gustavian style depends on good use of light and space, with painted furniture in pale colours.

In this cool green and white scheme (LEFT), the paintwork has been picked out in Adam green, giving the architectural features additional emphasis, and linking them to the woodwork on the landing beyond.

The ivory, yellow and pale smoke scheme (ABOVE) is almost Gustavian in style – light and bright without being too dominating. The panelling on the dado picks up the panelled features of the door, while the grey-painted furniture tones in with the overall style.

CHAPTER SEVEN

Children's Rooms

Since children grow at a rapid rate, whatever decorative scheme you envisage for a child's room will have to be changed with greater frequency than in most other rooms of the house. No self-respecting nine-year-old is going to share a room with teddybear curtains and wallpaper, and equally no teenager wants the images that a nine-year-old is happy with.

One practical solution to the need to change the decor in a child's room is to use a mixture of paper and paint, with a novelty papered dado area and plain paint or a simple small-print paper on the walls above. This has the double bonus that, when it comes to redecoration, you can probably get away with replacing the dado with a more suitable paper, and perhaps any border or frieze.

A patterned dado has the further advantage that it discourages spontaneous outbursts of graffiti, which are almost always executed within the height range of the perpetrators. The blank canvas of a plain wall proves irresistible to many small children!

If you use a vinyl or vinyl-coated wallcovering that is wipeable, you can remove any traces of their artwork and the accompanying black

Children like clutter, and a sense of fun or a quirky theme in their bedroom is comforting and sparks off their imagination. Here a coordinated range of children's bed linen and paper with a circus theme has been used as the starting point for the decorative scheme. The walls echo the cowslip ground of the circus fabric, while the paintwork takes up the blues in the print design. The individual motifs of the circus wallpaper frieze, which runs along the skirting board (baseboard), have been découpaged onto the bedhead, while the border to the paper frieze inspired the painted floor.

handprints. If you take the dado slightly higher than normal – to around l.2m (4ft) – it will help prevent any problems.

While most children enjoy lots of colour, pattern, and decoration, it does pay to be fairly flexible so that the scheme can be added to or altered in subtle ways in the interim stages of growing up, allowing wallspace for a new poster collection or shelves full of new toys. Displays of toys look terrific but do remember with very young children that friends visiting have a horrid habit of destroying your toddler's best-loved fire engine, so make sure that any easily dismantled or damaged toys are kept out of reach or out of sight. The actual objects that children accumulate are often colourful and fun in their own right, and it is worth planning some of these into the overall scheme so that they become a focal point rather than clashing with the rest of the room.

Stencilled or papered borders are really useful for adding colour and interest to the room and can be educational, telling a story or nursery rhyme, or showing the letters of the alphabet. There is a wide range of appealing borders available now in children's designs, including favourite characters from books, songs, and films.

There is nothing to stop you stencilling on fabric as well as on walls and furniture, and so you can add a motif that you have used for a border to a corner of a pillowcase for example. Shelves could have paper friezes or borders, though not for those where the children themselves are constantly taking objects from the shelf. The frieze or border would simply get damaged.

COLOUR CHOICES

Even small children have quite strong preferences for particular colours, and if these are rather odd, you can always use the colours to decorate smaller items of furniture. Bright colours are usually the most popular, but avoid making the room too bright. It can be very tiring to be surrounded by strong primary colours, and the room is one for sleeping in as well as playing. Soft but bright yellows and blues are always a good choice, but avoid too much pillarbox red. As

The circus theme of this deep border in a child's bedroom incorporates an attractive range of colours and some lively images, which lend themselves to other applications – for stencilling or découpaging on other pieces of furniture, or even fabric.

well as being rather hard, it is also difficult to get other colours to team well with it. Soft apricots and slightly dulled greens look good in combination, if jazzed up with attractive decorative elements.

The size of the window and the quality of light entering the room also help to determine the colour choice. If you are going for a blue and yellow scheme, in a room with cold north light, make sure that the yellow element is used for the larger areas.

TEENAGERS' ROOMS

Converting a room once occupied by a small child into one suitable for a teenager often demands a complete revamp of both the decoration scheme and quite a lot of the furniture. Again it pays to go for fairly plain large surfaces, since posters and other memorabilia often proliferate to the point of obliterating everything else.

Take out the bunkbed and put in a bed with a curtain, or put in a sofa bed to make it seem more grown-up – and they can use it when friends come to stay at weekends.

The images from the border on the far left have been cut out carefully and découpaged to the headboard of the painted wooden bed. Simple to execute, découpage is an excellent means of bringing life, colour and even humour to a child's room.

DECORATING FLOORS

Many people think of decorating the walls of their house, and perhaps the furniture, but stop short of decorating the floor. This is a pity, as it is a large area of the room and painting it is an interesting alternative to carpets. It can be as simple or elaborate as you like.

Hardboard flooring is probably about the cheapest surface to opt for and if you decorate it attractively, it can look every bit as good as carpet. Alternatively, if you have existing cork tiles you can jazz them up by painting them and then stencilling a border pattern.

There are various techniques you can use to create interesting effects on floors. If you are lucky enough to have good-quality wooden boards, these can be dealt with in a variety of ways. You can simply strip them and then varnish or polish them, or you can apply liming (pickling) paste or wax to them, which creates a paler bleached effect than the natural, slightly orangey tone of pine, one of the most commonly used flooring woods. The technique is very simple provided the floors have already been sanded and are clean and free of wax. You simply rub the liming (pickling) wax or paste in with fine-grade steel wool, leave it to dry off for about 20 minutes, and then buff it up with a duster. It works best as a finish on a wood with a raised grain, like pine or oak, as the white wax remains in the grooves, creating a white cast over the surface.

You can combine this with colourwashing (see pages 54–6) to produce a lightly coloured, pale surface. In this case you colourwash the wood first, and then lime (pickle) it afterwards. Colourwashing in pale blue or pale green, with a coat of liming wax over the top, looks particularly attractive. An alternative to colourwashing is to use one of the recently introduced colour stains that give a delicate pale tint to the wood and still allow the grain to show through.

Another option is to paint the floor with a thick matt paint (see Stockists and Suppliers for suggested types) and then varnish it to prevent it from chipping and scuffing. This gives a more attractive finish than simply applying a gloss paint. The advantage of painting the floor as opposed to liming it is that you do not need to strip the boards first, although you may well need to scrub them and then apply a coat of wooden primer first.

If, after you have varnished the paint, you use one of the proprietary antique floor polishes over the varnish, applied with steel wool and then buffed up with a duster, you will achieve an attractive soft glow that takes the hard shine off the varnish without spoiling the imperviousness of the surface.

(Depending on use, you may need to reapply varnish in two or three years.) Once you polish the floor you are then committed to polishing it on a regular basis rather than simply cleaning it with a damp sponge. Painting, varnishing, and waxing is an excellent method for rooms which receive only a modest amount of wear, such as bedrooms, dining rooms, or studies.

If you want a more decorated surface, you can paint freehand, or stencil a border or even an overall rug pattern effect, like a mosaic tile pattern, on the floor. The border is an attractive solution for a

OPPOSITE The design for the border to the painted floor has been copied and enlarged from the paper frieze. Templates have then been drawn out of cardboard and marked out in pencil on the floor area, before the floor has been painted in emulsion (latex) and then given several coats of hard-wearing matt varnish. Measuring and marking out a design like this so that it fits into the required area is the most complex part of the process, and has to be done carefully (see pages 104–5).

room which has a central square of carpet. You can take the theme for the pattern from some other element of decoration in the room, such as the bedlinen or the carpet pattern. In the child's room shown here, one element of the circus theme of the wallpaper border has been repeated as a surrounding border on the floor and the blind, while another motif – the clown – has been used to découpage the headboard of the bed and to make a mobile. Another decorative device if you have an attractive quilt is to take an element from the quilt design and recreate this elsewhere – as a stencilled border for curtains, for example, or above the cornice or skirting board.

PAINTING A FLOOR

If you are planning to create a stencilled border for a floor, or a stencilled floor pattern, you will not only need to transfer the design, but you will also have to work out how to make it fit the area you have in mind. Measure the floor area, with the help of a friend, using a ball of string. Draw the measurements out to scale on a sheet of squared (graph) paper, and mark in corners and awkward angles. Then measure the size of the stencil pattern you plan to use, and work out how best to organize it so that it fits the area you have in mind. You may need to experiment with the arrangement of the pattern in order to prevent ugly joins from occurring in the design at the corners of the room.

Before you start to stencil the pattern, clean the floor thoroughly, removing any wax with proprietary wax remover, to provide a good surface for the paint to adhere to. You can stencil directly onto floorboards, hardboard, lino, or cork tiles but the surface must be clean and grease- or wax-free before you start.

Once you have decided how to lay out the stencil pattern, mark off guidelines on the floor with chalk. Make sure, if you are creating a stencilled border, that the centre of one of the motifs lies in the centre of the main wall. For a stencilled rug, make certain that the entire rug is properly centred in the room, and that the pattern is centred on the rug itself.

Once you have marked out the floor, and have taped the first stencil in position, you can start to paint. There are various types of suitable paint, and the best to use for such a large area is flat oil-based paint or undercoat, or one of the new acrylic-based paints. They will need to be varnished afterwards with several coats of varnish to prevent chipping and scuffing. The modern water-based varnishes do not discolour, are hard-wearing, and have the advantage that the brushes can be cleaned out afterwards with water. They also dry quickly, which is important when working on a floor.

The central area of the floor has been painted in wide stripes in toning shades of yellow. The different techniques for creating stripes are explained on pages 130–1.

TECHNIQUES FOR STENCILLING A FLOOR

Make sure the floor is clean and grease-free (see page 26). Emulsion (latex) can be used, provided it is varnished afterwards. The pattern for the floor here was taken off the frieze, and enlarged.

You can use whatever pattern suits your room, but you will need to measure it out first. Before creating the pattern, give the floor a couple of coats of the base coat colour.

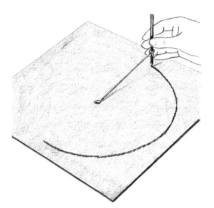

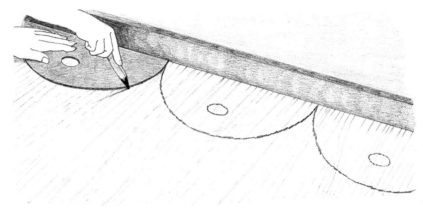

1 Make a template for the semi-circle by first drawing a large circle, using a drawing pin in the centre, and a pencil tied to a piece of string the length of half the diameter of the circle.

2 Cut the circle in half and use as a template. Position it on the floor and mark around it in pencil. Complete the pattern for the border.

3 Paint in the template pattern and then the stripe after masking off the template pattern as shown.

4 When you have completed the border, measure the area of the floor to determine the width of the roller stripes, and stick masking tape down to make a neat edge for the stripes. Paint between the masking tape strips. Leave to dry and then varnish with a couple of coats of varnish to make it hard wearing.

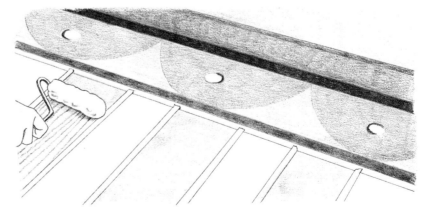

PAINTING A ROLLER BLIND

A plain roller blind (shade) can be given a facelift very easily by decorating it with a stencilled motif or by freehand painting. The stiff fabric used for roller blinds makes an ideal artists' canvas and you can use various paints to decorate it, including acrylics, emulsion paint, gouache, and fabric crayons. The choice of paint depends largely on what you have available and the size of the job, since artist's colours are more expensive than tinted household paints. The advantage of decorating your own blinds is that you can buy cheap, natural-coloured calico and paint and stiffen it yourself, if you wish. The plain off-white blinds known as hollands are ideal for a simple stencilled or stamped motif.

To create a simple border pattern, the same principles apply as for creating a border for a floor. You must find the centre point of the base of the blind and make sure that it forms the centre of your repeating pattern.

If you do not want to create a border, you can stencil, stamp, or paint a random design across the entire blind, taking the image from an existing pattern in the room. We chose a method in which a child could help, by colouring in the shapes with special fabric pens.

OPPOSITE It can be fun to involve children in the decoration of their own rooms. This simple border to a plain white roller blind (shade) has been painted on with special felt tips for painting on fabric. An adult can draw out the outline of the design – which was inspired by the wallpaper frieze – and the child can then colour in the shapes.

TRANSFERRING AN IMAGE TO A STENCIL

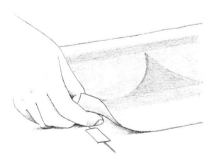

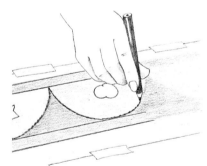

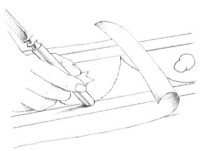

1 Take the pattern you have in mind – say from a piece of wallpaper or curtain fabric – and tape it flat to a work surface if possible. If it is on a piece of furniture, then work *in situ*. Spread a sheet of transparent paper over the design and tape it in position.

2 With a soft pencil, trace around the motif. Remove the tape and put the traced design, top side downwards, on a sheet of stencil cardboard.

3 Rub over the marked outline with a hard implement – the handle of a knife for example – so the pencil mark transfers to the cardboard underneath. Cut out the stencil in the usual way.

LEFT This warm-toned burgundy and sand scheme for a boy's room makes good use of an overall patterned paper to add warmth and novelty to the space. It contrasts well with the striped curtains in matching colours. The paintwork is picked out in the deep red. The eclectic mixture of traditional dark and light wood furniture adds an interesting touch.

ABOVE This fresh, light room for a small girl is decorative and pretty, without being overly fussy. The small print pattern of both the wallpaper and the curtain fabric gives the room intimacy, as does the display of wooden framed pictures above the bedhead. The elegant, white painted iron bed frame gives a characteristic Victorian accent.

ABOVE This children's bathroom has made imaginative use of a coordinated paper/paint decorative range, by cutting out the owl and pussy cat in a pea-green boat from the frieze and translating it into a carved-board bath surround. A simpler version would be to cut out the images and découpage them to the bath surround, varnishing well to ensure that it is waterproof.

OPPOSITE Equally imaginative is this richly decorated fireplace with its marvellous mixture of pattern and colour inspired by Moorish architecture. A door and shelf have been added to the fireplace to turn it into a cupboard. The decorative painting around it has transformed the cupboard into a Moorish castle, which is wonderful for games of soldiers as well as providing practical storage space. This is attractive without being too whimsical and would last from infancy to adolescence.

CHAPTER EIGHT

Bathrooms

It is only a matter of a few hundred years ago that bathrooms could be afforded by only the richest in the land – and not all of them wanted a bathroom. Chatsworth was one of the first grand houses to be fitted with bathrooms and the original bathrooms had extremely primitive plumbing and in some cases none at all.

The first baths, free-standing large copper tubs, were often partially concealed. They would be sited in an alcove, with thick curtains that could be pulled across to enclose the bather and give him or her some privacy, as well as protection from draughts.

In another version, the bath jutted out into the room with a tester above from which hung a circle of enclosing fabric – muslin in warmer climates and thick velvet in cooler ones.

Later on, in grander houses, the bathroom was part of a series of rooms, which included a dressing room and a water closet, and a room for the servants whose job it was to fill the bath by hand carrying large jugs of hot water from the kitchen boilers. In some smart homes, including Chatsworth, a special cupboard was built in a bedroom just for the bath.

Visually at least, we have started to return to this bygone era, with the bath sometimes situated in the middle of the room, or projecting into it from one wall, rather than being crammed against two walls in order to save space. The canopied bath popular in the eighteenth century would make a nice idea for a bathroom of any size and gives you plenty of scope to create exciting combinations of fabrics.

The deceptively simple decorative scheme for this country-style bathroom features pretty wallpaper in a pattern of stylized cartouches of roses in antique pink colours, with soft-coloured paintwork. A gingham blind (shade), a hardboard floor painted with wood graining, and a sponged bath add to the country look. A mosquito net over the bath provides an eccentric accent.

PLANNING THE BATHROOM

The bathroom deserves more careful planning than most rooms in the house, because the space is normally limited and specific functions have to be catered for, with some degree of comfort and warmth. The look of the bathroom is an important element in how comfortable it feels to use, as is the space you allocate to the various fittings, and how much room there is to use them. In many families a far larger number of people than the architect clearly imagined seem to cram into the bathroom together, to the point where everyone, including the family dog, seems to assemble there at the busiest point in the morning.

Storage space in the bathroom is important and needs to be carefully arranged so that the cupboard doors do not swing open to crack you on the head as you bend over the basin. It is also helpful if the various bottles that you require are near to hand since no one wants to have to clamber out of the bath to reach for the bath salts.

The amount of steam and condensation generated by most washing activities is considerable, and for any wallcovering to remain in good condition, it must be waterproof. This effectively means putting tiles around areas that are likely to get splashed, such as around the bath and basin, and in any shower area, and making sure that any paint or paper is water- or steam-resistant. Normally vinyl wallcoverings or vinyl-coated papers and/or oil- or acrylic-based paint should be used in the bathroom.

The bathroom fittings, even if old, do not necessarily have to be thrown out. There are many ways of renovating old baths, and the cupboards could perhaps be paint-finished to resemble marble, or subtly dragged or combed.

Hardwood can be used to surround the bath with a nice wide rim, and then wood-grained to look like much more expensive mahogany. Floors can be painted and then varnished to give a warmer, more homey feel than cold ceramic tiles.

Small bathrooms need a carefully unified decoration scheme if they are not to look even smaller. Pipework does not necessarily have to be boxed in – it can be painted instead and turned into an interesting architectural feature. The scale is extremely important in a small space, so steer away from large or overwhelming patterns for the walls. Try to make sure there are not too many different angles and shapes fighting with each other for dominance.

Bathroom windows are often neglected areas in the overall scheme, in part because in many houses they are glazed with frosted glass.

SPONGING TECHNIQUES

Sponging is one of the easiest paint-effect techniques to master and one of the quickest to execute. There are two ways to go about it. You can either cover a base coat of paint with a glaze (see page 24) – emulsion (latex), acrylic, or oil-based – and then use a sponge to dab off the glaze leaving a pleasingly mottled effect, or you can dab the glaze onto the base coat with a sponge. In both cases, a dampened sponge – water for emulsion (latex) and acrylic, white spirit (mineral spirits) or turpentine for oil-based glazes – will give a subtler, softer effect.

If you want to aim for a richer effect, you can sponge two colours, rather than just one, over the base coat. Try a mid-blue and mid-green over white, perhaps, or two shades of any colour over white.

As in all broken paint effects, the type of glaze you use plays an important part in the overall result, as does the choice of colours.

Since you are aiming for a subtle finish, it works best if the glaze is not too different tonally from the base coat, although by the time it is sponged the result on the wall will be much paler than the colour of the glaze in the tin, particularly when you are using oil-based glazes. A glaze that is very slightly darker than the base coat will give a translucent effect, whereas one that is lighter than the base coat will look more opaque.

Most paint experts recommend using an oil-based glaze because it gives the most professional-looking results. It is certainly easier to use the sponging-off technique with an oil-based glaze, as the emulsion and acrylic versions dry very quickly.

One of the virtues of broken paint effects is that the result does not have to look absolutely perfect. Half the charm of these paint-effect

A decorative wallpaper in soft colours can give warmth to a north-facing bathroom. This pink and white scheme is fresh without being in the least bit chilly. The paintwork is picked out in the taupe found in the wallpaper, adding a contemporary accent to this traditional wallpaper.

techniques stems from the slightly variable nature of the surface.

Remember when sponging any surface to keep the pressure as light and even as possible, and wipe the sponge clean or rinse it out in water or solvent, as appropriate, to avoid a build-up of paint and a clogged finish to the surface. The most professional-looking results are achieved by adhering to these principles.

You need very little in the way of equipment for sponging except a tray for the paint if you are sponging on, and a natural sponge for either technique (or, for sponging off, you could use a cellulose sponge which will create a more even, less subtle effect).

If you decide to work with two colours, sponge the first coat and allow it to dry before applying the second. When you do apply the second colour, try to apply the colour to the areas which are less obviously worked, and also try to overlap the previous coat of sponge marks. The aim is to keep the result as natural as possible, and it pays to use colours that are not too dissimilar in tone. Clear polyurethane varnish, applied once the paint is completely dry, will make the surface waterproof.

HOW TO SPONGE ON

1 Apply the base coat – emulsion (latex) or eggshell – taking care to create an even finish.

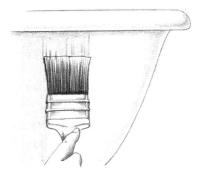

2 Prepare the glaze (emulsion-based for an emulsion base coat and oil-based for an eggshell base coat) and put it in a tray. Mix any colours required as appropriate (see page 24).

3 Wring the sponge out in water for emulsion glaze, or in turpentine or white spirit (mineral spirits) for oil-based glaze.

4 Dip the sponge in the paint and then wipe it on a rag, if necessary, to remove some of the paint. Apply the sponge on the painted surface using light, dabbing movements.

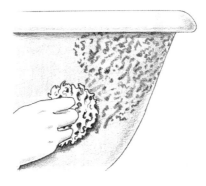

5 Wring the sponge out frequently to avoid a build-up of paint.

6 When you get to the corners of the room, apply the glaze coat of paint fairly thinly and strip a bit off the sponge so that you can work into the awkward angles of the corner easily, otherwise you will get an unattractive tide mark at the edges.

7 If you are sponging on a second colour, wait for the first to dry before applying the second.

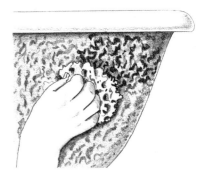

HOW TO SPONGE OFF

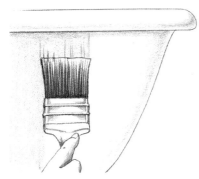  

1 Apply the base coat (as for Sponging On). If you are using quick-drying emulsion or acrylic paint, work in smallish squares to ensure that you keep a wet edge to the paint (in other words, the edges must not dry out).

2 Wring the sponge out in water or white spirit (mineral spirits), as appropriate, and start to dab the glaze off the surface.

3 Continue along the surface, working in squares and cleaning the sponge at regular intervals.

The sides of this antique claw-footed roll-top bath have been sponged in a taupe glaze over a white ground. A scroll pattern, taken from the wallpaper, has been added around the base of the bath in the pink colour of the wallpaper.

WOOD GRAINING

One of the most refined of the decorator's arts is that of wood graining. It is a technique that has long been used to imitate expensive and exotic woods, from mahogany to burr walnut and tortoiseshell. Wood graining is particularly useful if you want a new piece of furniture to blend in with existing older pieces. True wood-graining skills are beyond the scope of most amateurs, but decorative wood graining is far simpler and just as effective in most situations.

The easiest woods to copy are pine, oak, and maple, which all have a distinct graining pattern. Although you may wish to simulate the colour of the wood exactly, it looks attractive if you use a colour, such as dusty blue or olive green, with the result that the surface resembles stained rather than natural wood.

The base coat over which you apply the glaze is always lighter. Once it is dry, you apply the glaze with a brush and work into it while it is still wet to produce the grained pattern. The pattern can be created in a variety of ways, but the simplest for oak- or pine-type effects is to use a purpose-made rocker. This constitutes a rubber tool with a comb-like pattern which you drag through the wet paint. Wherever you pause, you will get a knot-like effect imitating the grain marks. Once you have created this initial pattern, you can brush it over lightly with a soft-bristled brush to make it look more subtle.

OPPOSITE This washbasin cabinet has been decoratively woodgrained in a pale taupe shade, using the same technique as for the floor. A thinnish glaze is applied over a paler ground, and is then dragged through with a graining rocker.

LEFT Graining rocker and glaze.

If you do not want to go to the trouble of imitating a wood-grain pattern, you can opt for a simple version – combing – which simply makes regular vertical lines in the glaze, rather like a more exaggerated form of dragging (see pages 84–8). Combing, like dragging and wood-graining, is worked using a wet glaze over a dry base coat.

A variety of implements can be used for combing, but a broad-toothed purpose-made rubber comb is normally employed. You can create many different patterns – criss-cross, moiré, shell, or wave versions are all popular. The size and spacing of the comb you choose will determine the effect of the pattern that is created. The combs may be made of steel, rubber, or plastic, or you could make your own from stiff cardboard sealed with varnish.

WOOD-GRAINING TECHNIQUES

1 Clean the surface thoroughly, removing any grease or wax with a proprietary cleaner.

2 Apply a pale base coat of eggshell paint, if necessary matching as closely as possible the wood effect you are aiming to imitate.

3 Once the base coat is completely dry, brush on the glaze in a shade slightly darker than the base coat.

4 Using the rocker, drag it firmly and evenly down the wet glazed surface. Stop the movement wherever you want a "knot" effect to appear.

5 Repeat the process next to the first line of grain marks, staggering the knot marks so that they do not appear to be in a regular line.

6 When dry, varnish with a water-based varnish to seal. Once the varnish is completely dry, apply a second coat of varnish to provide a complete seal.

COMBING

As a decorative paint effect, combing is relatively easy to carry out and does not require any special skill or tools, apart from a toothed comb, normally made from rubber or plastic, and bought from any good decorating shop. Alternatively, you can construct your own from heavy-duty cardboard if you prefer.

The teeth of the comb are dragged through the wet glazed surface which has been applied over a dry, eggshell base coat, with the result that the base coat shows through in a series of even lines, rather like dragging, but more pronounced. The pattern can vary from simple lines of combing, to basketweave (as shown below) or wave patterns. If you vary the direction of the marks, it will add interest to the surface. If you comb a floor, you will need to varnish it afterwards to make it wearproof.

COMBING TECHNIQUES

1 Paint on an eggshell base coat, then rub it down lightly after it is dry. Apply a rough coat of glaze.

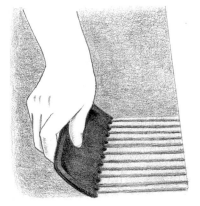

2 With the glaze still wet, drag a comb through the surface, keeping the strokes even.

3 Make a basketweave pattern by creating both horizontal and vertical dragging lines in a squared pattern.

The classic decorating colour scheme of blue and white looks fresh and pretty in a bathroom, and here, a simple coordinating range of blue-and-white papers, borders, and tiles has been used for the decoration. The shell motif has been carried onto the bath itself in the form of a stencil and the floor has been stripped, limed (pickled), and waxed. The borders have been used to frame the walls themselves, running both horizontally and vertically around the wall edges. Shells collected from the beach and blue-and-white china add simple but stylish finishing touches to the scheme.

LEFT This small bathroom with steps leading into it has the feeling of the cabin of a boat, or a beach hut. The simple striped wallpaper, reminiscent of deckchair canvas, as well as the rattan furnishings, shell-motif fabric, and matching wallpaper border, all add to this impression. The whole scheme is unified by limiting the colour palette to blue, taupe and white.

OPPOSITE Rough-plastered walls and bleached floorboards stencilled with a small repeat motif and border pattern in faded earth pigments are perfectly in keeping with the centuries-old feel of this cloakroom, in which even the basin does not seem incongruous. The stencils were inspired by a Provencal woodblock, and the faded terracotta, ochre, and dove grey palette are also redolent of Provence.

CHAPTER NINE

Halls and Stairs

T he most difficult parts of the house to decorate, these areas present quite a challenge to the interior decorator. Lack of light, high ceilings, and heavy wear and tear all demand special solutions. If you add to that the fact that there is little else to draw your attention, you are faced with a complex set of problems to solve in design terms.

The first task is to assess the architectural merits, and defects. In most cases, the real problem is that the hallway is long, dark, and narrow, and you need to find decorating schemes that will improve the feeling of light and space. Ideally, since so many other rooms open off these areas, you need to find some way of linking the design to those of the other rooms in the house, by repeating either colour schemes or specific motifs, or repeating the floor covering throughout the space, be it plain boards or carpets.

If you opt for pattern on the walls, then it might be advisable to go either for texture – in the form of an embossed, hard-wearing, wipable wallpaper or a simple sprig or lattice pattern wallpaper – or for a stippled paint finish, or subtle geometric pattern, in the form of toning stripes or a geometric, randomly printed stencil or block pattern. A panelled dado area, or one covered in embossed

Brown roller stripes on a white wall, emphasized by a red and green stencilled border and spongeware plates, give this hallway the look of a country cottage. The sponge effect of the roller was responsible for the soft, textured effect of the stripes, providing an appropriate backdrop for antique country furniture, baskets, trugs, and flowers.

wallcovering (see page 41), will help solve some of the problems of wear and tear, since painted plaster in hallways and on stairwells is easily chipped as large objects are manhandled around the house.

The stairwell is particularly at risk from trails of sticky or dirty handprints in a family home, as young children tend to use the walls to support themselves when going up and down stairs. A durable, wipable paper on the dado area, or at the least a gloss-painted finish to this height would save a lot of unnecessary redecoration.

If you do not have the budget or inclination for matching carpet throughout this area, and it receives the most wear of any carpet in the house, thereby forcing you to buy the most expensive, then opt for stripped floors instead. If you do not like the idea of plain boards, patterns can be stencilled as a border which can be continued up the stair treads as well.

Subtle patterns work best in inky blues or olive greens, and the boards can be limed (pickled) to give a soft, pale sheen to the area, which also gives the stencilled pattern an attractive antique quality. You will need to varnish the area to protect the surface. This means that if you go for liming (pickling) you will have to use a wax-free liming (pickling) paste rather than the more commonly used liming (pickling) wax, which cannot be varnished afterwards.

Remember that the hallway is the first impression visitors get of the house, and probably the most lasting one. A dim and dingy hallway, no matter how well decorated the rest of the house is, creates a depressing atmosphere. Most hallways have a large number of doors opening off them, and one solution to this problem is to find ways of making an interesting feature of them, possibly by taking a stencilled border around the architrave or by giving the doors attractive paint finishes, such as dragging, combing, or wood graining.

A picture rail will help to reduce the height of a particularly high-ceilinged hall, and will also help it to appear wider by bringing the ceiling down lower visually.

On a purely practical note, remember that when decoration is being undertaken, you will need to erect a safe, stable working platform with ladders and boards to reach the ceilings and higher parts of the wall above the stair well.

OPPOSITE The roller stripes have been taken up to dado (chair) rail height on the stairs, and up to picture rail height in the hall. The stencilled border is above the dado rail on the stairs but below the picture rail, creating a mirror image effect which suits the relative proportions of the two areas. (The addition of a thin brown horizontal stripe was necessary to make a bridge between the roller stripes and the picture rail.) Consider the dimensions of the walls carefully before deciding where to position borders, and do not be afraid to ring the changes, as we have done in this hall and stairway.

HALLWAY TECHNIQUES

Stripes are one of the most attractive patterned effects. Perennially elegant, they can be used in a variety of ways: as all-over decoration or as small bands or borders to define an area, such as a window or door frame. Vertical stripes will add height; horizontal stripes will reduce it, and you can use this attribute to lower or raise apparent ceiling heights.

Some of the best colour schemes for stripes involve slightly unusual colour combinations:

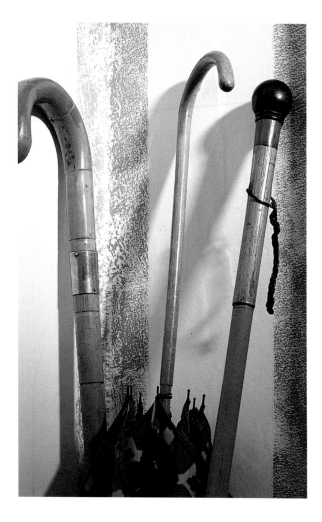

misty taupe and parma violet, or ochre and terracotta. Steer clear of very strong contrasts – dark red and white, dark green and white – as these, particularly if the stripes are broad, would be difficult to live with and certainly difficult to decorate around. You would need a very sure eye to make this work with other patterns and colours, and the effect could easily dominate the room.

You can choose simple, broad, even stripes, created quickly and simply with a roller; or go for a more formal look, in which the stripes are carefully measured, and the paint is applied in neatly masked-off stripes, using architect's tape to keep the vertical or horizontal line. Using this latter technique, you would not necessarily have to go for evenly spaced stripes, but could vary the stripe width and the colours. Be warned, though: it will take far longer than these relatively quick and simple roller stripes.

The mottled texture of the roller stripes is achieved by painting with fairly thick, undiluted paint and by not overloading the roller with paint.

CREATING ROLLER STRIPES

The best effect is achieved using emulsion (latex) paint and a narrower than normal roller. For the stripes in this hallway, a roller about 23cm (9in) wide was used. If you cannot buy a smaller one easily, cut down an existing roller to size.

The paint should be fairly thick and applied to the wall in one single application. In other words, do not run the roller back and forth but work in one continuous movement from top to bottom of the wall.

Use two different colours, like pale blue and and a soft tobacco brown. Simply paint one wall with the stripes of one colour, making each stripe a roller's width apart, and then paint the second colour between the first stripes. The paint will overlap slightly in places where your line slightly veers off the vertical, but the aim of this kind of stripe is for effect, not perfection. If you want perfection, then carry it out using masking tape to separate the colours.

The only real problem you face using this roller stripe technique is how to get into any corners, and what to do where the walls butts up to another right-angled surface. The simplest solution if you don't want to paint these areas with a brush is to stop the stripes and add a decorative border.

To finish off the effect here, the roller stripes had a simple self-coloured 2.5cm (1in) border added, and a stencilled border was then painted above the striped area, and also above the dado rail (chair rail) on the stairs.

ROLLER STRIPE TECHNIQUES

1 Turn the paint – ideally a non-drip emulsion – into a roller tray and load the roller, taking care not to get too much paint on the roller (see Roller Painting, step 2).

2 Starting at the top of the area, run the roller down the wall, without going over the surface more than once, to give a textured paint finish.

3 Create a neat edge at the top of the roller stripes by masking off with architect's tape a 2.5cm (1in) border before the paint is applied.

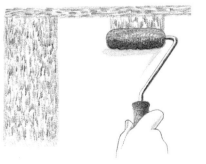

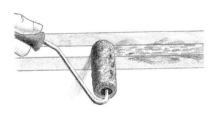

STENCILLING A BORDER

Stencilling is one of the most useful techniques in the home decorator's repertoire, since it creates exciting pattern almost anywhere it is required – around doorways and windows; in panels on shutters, screens and doors; on walls and furniture; and even on fabric.

Originated by the Chinese before 3000BC, stencilling was used in Europe from the sixth century AD. It continued to gain popularity and was widely used in Britain by the Middle Ages, particularly on the walls of churches. By Tudor times, stencilling was also decorating the walls of large manor houses, and it had become highly popular by the eighteenth century. In the nineteenth century, however, it was once more reserved mainly for churches, until the Arts and Crafts and Gothic Revival movements increased interest in it once more. Wallpaper was still expensive and stencilling provided a useful means of repeating patterns on walls to make them look as if they were papered. In fact, stencilling was used as the means of decorating these early papers, along with hand blocking.

The taste for, and popularity of, stencilling was by no means confined to the British Isles, and the early settlers in America used it in abundance to decorate their homesteads. The images used tended to be those of their domestic life – baskets of apples, bowls of flowers – and were used to decorate furniture, floors, doors, and even bed linen. Whole rooms would be stencilled, with the walls completely covered in decorative stencilled patterns.

The secret of successful stencilling is not only to choose an appropriate pattern, but also to make sure that the colours are not too garish. Any stencil looks much more attractive if the colours are soft and not too evenly applied. Half the charm of stencilling comes from the slightly idiosyncratic marks made. If you find you have created too bright and strong a stencil pattern, you can always give it an instantly aged appearance, by rubbing over it when it is dry with some fine-gauge steel wool to remove the paint, or painting a thin wash of diluted emulsion (latex) – either white or off white – or tinted matt varnish to knock the colour back.

Another factor in making sure the stencil looks appropriate is proportion. This can be very difficult to gauge, but too narrow and thin a border, or a border positioned too high on the wall, can spoil the overall effect.

A solution is to take your stencil card and colour in a few repeats on paper, using children's paints or crayons, and then cut these out and fix them to the wall in the chosen position. In this way you can test out both the colour and the scale to see if it looks right. If it is too small, you can enlarge the stencil yourself simply by taking an enlarged photocopy and cutting another stencil card (see page 134).

Make sure the chosen colours look good for the motif you are using. The kind of traditional motifs used in early American stencils were generally painted in soft, natural colours derived from local pigments – earthy browns, rusty reds, and soft blues and greens. Vibrant shades would look completely out of place.

Stencilled borders can be used both to emphasize architectural features and to make up for the lack of them. Look carefully at the room and see what natural shapes and lines it possesses. Casement windows, alcoves, and sloping walls can all be emphasized with stencil patterns, just as a room without cornices, picture rails or dado rails (chair rails) can have stencilled borders added at these heights to break up an otherwise box-like area.

In other words, stencilling is hard work, particularly when doing a border near a ceiling where your arms are above your head. It is much easier to stencil a pattern at dado height!

If you are considering using a lot of stencil pattern, make sure that it suits the rest of the decor. Too many decorative elements fighting against each other will simply cancel each other out and destroy the impact.

Stencilled patterns in areas that are likely to receive a lot of wear should be protected with a coat of multi-purpose varnish, such as a polyurethane one that is matt and invisible, and does not yellow with age.

The stencilled border above the dado (chair) rail illustrates the way the two colours have been used – a dark red forms the centre part of the design and a soft green has been used for the edges. The juxtaposition of these two colours alongside the brown adds depth and interest.

HOW TO STENCIL

Experts adopt many ways of applying stencils, and stencilling can be done using several different media. Lyn le Grice, one of the best-known stencilling experts, favours the use of car spray paint for hers, which gives a gently mottled but very professional-looking finish. If you are prepared to put up with the smell given off by this type of paint, and the fact that the area surrounding the stencils needs a lot of careful masking off, then use a spray paint.

If, however, you prefer something a little less problematic, stencil paint (which is specially formulated so that it is fairly dry and does not seep under the bridge of the stencil card) is ideal, as are the stencil crayons you can now buy.

In order to copy an existing motif in your decorating scheme, you may prefer to cut your own stencil pattern rather than buy one ready-made, although some very attractive ready-made ones can now be found.

If, though, you wish to take a motif from some existing wallpaper or fabric, for example, then trace it off. Turn the tracing over, and go over the back of the pattern with a soft pencil. Then turn it right side up again, place it on the stencil card, and rub over the stencil pattern with a coin to transfer the pattern onto the stencil card beneath. Once it has been transferred, cut around the pattern carefully using a very sharp knife, such as a craft knife.

Attention to detail is the key to success in any decorative scheme. Here the china on display echoes the colour range and design style of the paint effects. You can use a collection of china to determine a paint effect or colour scheme, or you can work in the opposite direction, and hunt out china, glassware, or other ornaments to match the scheme you have in mind. A collection of blue and white china would look good with blue and white painted stripes, while shells, driftwood, and wooden bowls could be accompanied by natural-coloured stripes in ivory and cream, with some simple prints to add a little colour. Brighter stripes could be used with an array of coloured glass.

To create a good strong stencil design, the pattern must have plenty of bridges (linking areas of cardboard) to hold it together. Too few of these, and the stencil will buckle or tear with use, which is why stencil patterns are rather simplistic, in general. If you are planning a border, cut small registration marks in each corner of the stencil so that you can line it up correctly to make a repeating pattern. Make sure there is plenty of extra cardboard around the design, so that you do not inadvertently paint over the edges onto the wall or furniture underneath.

PREPARATION AND PAINTING

 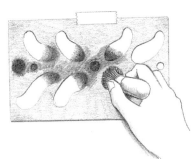 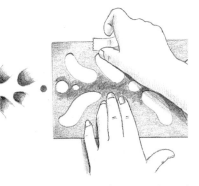

1 Make sure the surface you wish to stencil is clean and dry. Position the stencil where you want it, either using masking tape to hold it in position or by lining up registration marks (small notches in the stencil border), after checking it is straight using a T-square. (Professionals simply hold it in place.)

2 Dip the stencil brush in your chosen colour and pounce the brush briefly on paper to distribute the paint evenly. Then pounce it through the stencil card until all the gaps are filled with colour. Pouncing involves dabbing the brush in an up and down motion.

3 Leave to dry for a few seconds and then peel off the tape. Reapply the stencil to the next part of the border, lining up any registration marks to make sure the pattern is complete.

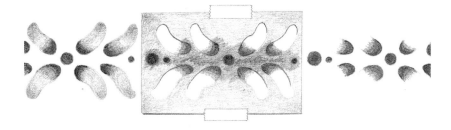

4 If you are using more than one colour, apply the first colour to the entire border and allow to dry before adding the next colour.

5 Once the entire stencilled area is dry, you can varnish it, if desired, with a coat of clear polyurethane varnish.

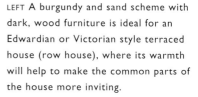

LEFT A burgundy and sand scheme with dark, wood furniture is ideal for an Edwardian or Victorian style terraced house (row house), where its warmth will help to make the common parts of the house more inviting.

LEFT When using strong colour, as in this jade green painted hallway, it pays to keep the other detailing very simple, so that the paint colour becomes the focal point.

OPPOSITE An elegant pale taupe and white painted hallway provides a sophisticated backdrop for the wide staircase with its elegant wrought iron bannister detail. Strong colour contrasts, in the wall hangings and hall table cover, provide the visual interest.

OVERLEAF A hallway with several doors opening from it, and with interesting architectural features, is often best given a bold but simple treatment, as with this lavender-blue painted hallway. An oriental rug provides the link between the dark wood of the furniture, the paint colour and the wooden floor.

STOCKISTS AND SUPPLIERS

UNITED KINGDOM

J.W.Bollom
13 Theobald's Road
London WC1X 8FN
0171-242 0313
General painting supplies
314 Old Brompton Road
London SW5 9JH
(Showroom)

C.Brewers
327 Putney Bridge Road
London SW15 2PG
0181-788 9335
General painting supplies.
Various branches
in S.E. England

Brodie and Middleton Ltd
68 Drury Lane
London WC2B 5SP
0171-836 3289
Pigments and paints

Cornelissen and Son Ltd
105 Great Russell Street
London WC1B 3RY
0171-636 1045
Pigments and brushes

Craig & Rose plc
172 Leith Walk
Edinburgh EH6 5ER
0131-554 1131
Glazes, specialist brushes.
Stockists nationwide.

Daler-Rowney Limited
PO Box 10
Southern Industrial Estate
Bracknell
Berkshire
RG12 8ST
01344-424621
Artists' materials

The Dover Bookshop
18 Earlham Street
London WC2H 9LN
0171-836 2111
Specialist books of scraps and borders for découpage

The English Stamp Company
Sunnydown
Worth Matravers
Dorset BH19 3JP
01929-439117

Farrow & Ball
Uddens Trading Estate
Wimbourne
Dorset BH21 7NL
01202-876141
National Trust range of historical paints

Foxell & James Ltd,
57 Farringdon Road
London EC1M 3JH
0171-405 0152
Varnishes, primers, paints, glazes, floor finishes, rabbit-skin glue, whiting, metal powders

Green & Stone
259 Kings Road
London SW3 5EL
0171-352 0837
Artists' materials

W.Habberley Meadows Ltd
5 Saxon Way
Chelmsley Wood
Birmingham B37 5AY
0121-770 2905
Artists' paints and brushes, gilding materials

Hawkin & Co
Saint Margaret
Harlestone
Norfolk IP20 0PJ
01986-782 536
Mail order découpage scraps

J.T.Keep & Co
13 Theobalds Road
London WC1X 8SN
0171-242 7578
General decorating suppliers

Lyn Le Grice Stencil Design Ltd
The Stencil House
53 Chapel Street,
Penzance
Cornwall TR18 4AS
01736-64193
Stencil books, kits and materials

E.Milner Oxford Ltd
Clanville Road
Cowley
Oxford OX4 2DB
01865-718171
General painting supplies

John Myland
80 Norwood High Street
London SE27 9NW
0181-670 9161
Artists' brushes and materials

Paint Magic
116 Sheen Road
Richmond
TW9 1UR
0181-940 5503
Paint effect kits, colourwash, woodwash, crackle glaze, stencilling supplies

The Paint Service Co. Ltd
19 Eccleston Street
London SW1W 9LX
0171-730 6408

Pavilion Stencils
6a Howe Street
Edinburgh EH3 6TD
0131-225 3590
Stencilling supplies

E.Ploton Ltd
273 Archway Road
London N6 5AA
0181-348 0315
Metallic powders, gilding materials

Potmolen Paint
27 Woodcock Industrial Estate
Warminster
Wiltshire BA12 9DX
01985-213960
Paints and finishes suitable for old buildings

J.H.Ratcliffe & Co. (Paints) Ltd
135a Linaker Street
Southport PR8 5DF
01704-537999
Transparent oil glaze

The Shaker Shop
25 Harcourt Street
London W1H 1DT
0171-724 7672
Old Village buttermilk paints

Stuart R. Stevenson
68 Clerkenwell Road
London EC1M 5QA
0171-253 1693
Gilding materials

UNITED STATES

Decorating Centers
1555 Third Avenue
New York
NY 10028
(212) 289-6300

2475 Broadway
New York
NY 10025
(212) 769-1440

Sam Flax
12 West 20th Street
New York
NY 10011
(212) 620-3038

425 Park Avenue
New York
NY 10022
(212) 620-3060

Liberty Paint Co.
969 Columbia Street
Hudson
NY 12534
(518) 828-4060

Pearl Paint Co.
308 Canal Street
New York
NY 10013
(212) 431-7932

Wolf Paper and Paint
Janovic Plaza
771 Ninth Avenue
New York
NY 10019
(212) 245-3241

Janovic Plaza
1150 Third Avenue
New York
NY 10022
(212) 772-1400

UNITED KINGDOM

LONDON SHOPS
Brent Cross (clothes only) 0181 202 2679
Chelsea 0171 823 7550
Covent Garden 0171 240 1997
Ealing 0181 579 5197
Kensington 0171 938 3751
Knightsbridge (clothes only) 0171 823 9700
Knightsbridge (home furnishings only) 0171 235 9797
Marble Arch 0171 355 1363
Oxford Circus 0171 437 9760

COUNTRY SHOPS
Aberdeen 01224 625787
Aylesbury 01296 84574
Banbury 01295 271295
Barnet 0181 449 9866
Bath 01225 460341
Bedford 01234 211416
Belfast 01232 233313
Beverley 01482 872444
Birmingham 0121 631 2842
Bishops Stortford 01279 655613
Bournemouth (clothes only) 01202 293764
Brighton 01273 205304
Bristol, Broadmead 0117 9221011
Bristol, Clifton 0117 9277468
Bromley 0181 290 6620
Bury St Edmunds 01284 755658
Cambridge 01223 351378
Canterbury 01227 450961
Cardiff 01222 340808
Carlisle 01228 48810
Chelmsford 01245 359602
Cheltenham 01242 580770
Chester (clothes only) 01244 313964
Chester (home furnishings only) 01224 316403
Chichester 01243 775255
Colchester 01206 562692
Derby 01332 361642
Dudley 01384 79730
Eastbourne 01323 411955
Edinburgh (clothes only) 0131 225 1218
Edinburgh (home furnishings only) 0131 225 1121
Epsom 01372 739595
Exeter 01392 53949
Farnham 01252 712812
Gateshead 0191 493 2411
Glasgow 0141 226 5040
Guildford 01483 34152
Harrogate 01423 526799
Heathrow 0181 759 1951
Hereford 01432 272446
High Wycombe 01494 442394
Hitchin 01462 420445
Horsham 01403 259052
Ipswich 01473 216828
Ipswich 01473 721124
Isle of Man 01624 801213
Jersey 01534 608084

Kings Lynn 01553 768881
Kingston 0181 549 0055
Leamington Spa 01926 314584
Leeds 0113 2450622
Leicester 0116 2513165
Lincoln 01522 511611
Llanidloes 01686 412557
Maidstone 01622 750138
Manchester 0161 834 7335
Middlesbrough 01642 226034
Milton Keynes 01908 660190
Newcastle-Under-Lyme 01782 662014
Newport I.O.W. 01983 821806
Northampton (clothes only) 01604 231975
Norwich 01603 632958
Nottingham 0115 9503366
Oxford 01865 791689
Perth 01738 623141
Peterborough 01733 311766
Plymouth 01752 268344
Preston 01772 202425
Reading 01734 594313
Richmond 0181 940 9556
Salisbury 01722 338383
Sheffield 0114 2701855
Sheffield Meadowhall 01742 568221
Shrewsbury 01743 351467
Skipton 01756 700301
Solihull 0121 704 4344
Southampton 01703 228944
Southport 01704 546214
St Albans 01727 864611
Stockport 0161 474 7927
Stratford-Upon-Avon 01789 298852
Sutton 0181 643 9790
Sutton Coldfield 0121 355 3671
Swindon 01793 641727
Taunton 01823 288202
Tenterden 01580 765188
Torquay 01803 291443
Truro 01872 223019
Tunbridge Wells 01892 534431
Watford 01923 254411
Wilmslow 01625 535331
Winchester 01962 855716
Windsor (clothes only) 01753 854345
Windsor (home furnishings only) 01753 831456
Wolverhampton 01902 27293
Worcester 01905 20177
Worthing 01903 205160
Yeovil 01935 79863
York 01904 627707

REPUBLIC OF IRELAND SHOPS
Cork 00 35 32 127 4070
Dublin 00 35 31 679 5433

HOMEBASES
Within Sainsbury's Homebase House and Garden Centres
Basildon 01268 584088
Basingstoke 01256 469510
Bath 01225 339293

Blackheath 0181 856 9767
Bradford 01274 611929
Branksome 01202 768311
Brentford 0181 847 2214
Camberley 01276 686227
Cardiff 01222 499675
Catford 0181 461 0606
Chelmsford 01245 257257
Chichester 01243 533373
Colchester 01206 869187
Coventry 01203 715901
Crawley 01293 538351
Crayford 01322 558614
Croydon 0181 684 8250
Derby 01332 291260
Enfield 0181 366 2236
Gloucester 01452 526806
Guildford 01483 304115
Harlow 01279 413355
Hatfield 01707 275837
Hendon 0181 200 7737
Hull 01482 572434
Ilford 0181 590 0212
Ipswich 01473 721124
Kensington 0171 603 2285
Kingston 0181 949 7861
Leeds 01132 685010
Leicester 01162 546075
Luton 0582 593445
Maidstone 01622 715400
Mill Hill 0181 203 7740
Milton Keynes 01908 692727
New Southgate 0181 368 1698
Newcastle-Under-Lyme 01782 711752
Northampton 01604 234143
Norwich 01603 417474
Nottingham 01159 413885
Oldbury 0121 544 7333
Orpington 01689 890353
Oxford 01865 747979
Penge 0181 778 4214
Rayleigh Weir 01268 745374
Reading 01734 584572
Richmond 0181 876 2235
Rochester 01634 200088
Romford 01708 730326
Sheffield 01742 555175
Southampton 01703 510098
Stockport 0161 474 7489
Swansea 01792 650935
Swindon 01793 487125
Tunbridge Wells 01892 546646
Wakefield 01924 387011
Walsall 01922 29524
Walsgrave 01203 602086
Waltham Cross 01992 625275
Walthamstow 0181 531 8233
Watford 01923 252075
Willesden 0181 459 3989
Wimbledon 0181 946 9802
Worcester 01905 420401
Worle 01934 512628
York 01904 643911

UNITED STATES OF AMERICA
Albany 518 452 4998

Ann Arbor 313 747 6620
Annapolis 410 268 6906
Ardmore 215 896 8293/0208
Arlington 703 415 2111
Atlanta-Lenox 404 231 0685
Atlanta-Perimeter 404 395 6027
Austin 512 451 4036
Bal Harbour 305 864 5628
Beachwood 216 831 7621
Birch Run 517 624 9297
Birmingham 205 985 0090
Bluffton 803 837 2366
Boca Raton 407 368 5622
Boston 617 536 0505
Bridgewater 908 725 3700
Buffalo 716 681 8600
Burlington/Boston 617 272 4540
Burlington/Vermont 802 658 5006
Cambridge 617 576 3690
Carmel-by-the-Sea 408 624 8095
Central Valley 914 928 4561
Charleston 803 723 3967
Charlotte 704 362 0926
Charlottesville 804 971 7707
Chattanooga 615 855 5496
Chestnut Hill 617 965 7640
Chestnut Hill 215 242 9262
Chicago 312 951 8004
Cincinnati 513 793 5535
Columbus 614 224 5057
Corte Madera 415 924 5770
Costa Mesa 714 545 9322
Cranston 401 946 1211
Dallas-Galleria 214 980 9858
Dallas Northpark 214 369 5755
Danbury 203 790 5068
Dayton 513 299 9007
Denver 303 571 0050
Denver-Cherry Creek 303 322 9401
Des Moines 515 243 8881
Destin 904 654 2626
Edina 612 920 2811
Fairfax 703 352 7960
Farmington 203 521 8967
Fort Lauderdale 305 563 2300
Fort Worth 817 346 4666
Freeport 207 865 3300
Germantown 901 756 7036
Gilroy 408 848 5470
Glendale 818 242 0428
Grand Rapids 616 942 6828
Greenville 302 575 1653
Greenwich 203 661 5678
Grosse Pointe 313 886 6960
Hackensack 201 488 0130
Hingham 617 740 4122
Honolulu 808 942 5200
Houston 713 871 9669
Houston/West Oaks 713 558 6113 +971 9669 +622 2262
Indianapolis 317 848 9855
Jacksonville 904 358 7548
Jeffersonville 614 948 2016
Kansas City 816 931 0731
King of Prussia 610 354 9137
Knoxville 615 558 6385
Lake Forest 708 615 1405